The Final Season

Nigel McCrery was educated at Trinity College, Cambridge and has a long-standing interest in military history. He has written several books about the First World War, including *All the King's Men*, the true story of George V's own Sandringham Company which disappeared during the conflict. The book became a major BBC film starring David Jason and Maggie Smith and achieved the second biggest BBC drama audience of all time. Nigel has also created and written a number of prime-time BBC dramas including *Born and Bred*, *Touching Evil*, *Back-up*, *Impact*, *Silent Witness* and *New Tricks*.

Praise for *The Final Season*

Fascinating…For those of us who love football, and still more for those who make fortunes playing it, all this sacrifice should offer considerable food for thought. Gary Lineker says as much in a thoughtful foreword…I wish with all my heart a copy could be given to every Premier League player.   *Daily Mail*

D0300616

The Final Season

The Footballers Who Fought and
Died in the Great War

Nigel McCrery

arrow books

1 3 5 7 9 10 8 6 4 2

Arrow Books
20 Vauxhall Bridge Road
London SW1V 2SA

Arrow Books is part of the Penguin Random House group of companies
whose addresses can be found at global.penguinrandomhouse.com.

Penguin
Random House
UK

First published by Random House Books in 2014
First published in paperback by Arrow Books in 2015

www.randomhouse.co.uk

A CIP catalogue record for this book is
available from the British Library.

ISBN 9780099594666

Printed and bound in Great Britain by CPI Group (UK) Ltd, Croydon, CR0 4YY

Contents

Foreword

Over the course of the First World War, Britain lost over half a million men in the prime of life. But although each and every death was a tragedy, the sad fact is that outside the immediate circle of their family and friends most of these men became almost anonymous; another name on the ever-growing casualty lists in the papers.

Some deaths, however, were noticed by the general public. Sportsmen were some of the greatest stars of the day, and none were more important to people than the players on their local football team. These men were heroes of the crowd, exemplifying commitment, dedication and teamwork to the fans who gathered every Saturday to watch them play. And, like the other healthy young men of their generation, when the need of their country was great they exchanged the colours of their team strip for the khaki of a soldier's uniform. They left behind the adulation of the crowds in the stands and went to face deprivation and danger on the battlefields of France and Belgium.

Well-known as they were, the deeds and sacrifices of these brave men were widely reported at the time. Imagine, if you can, the entire back four of your favourite team being killed in a single day; on the following day, your star striker and that promising new winger. As astonishing as it seems, the casualties that occurred in theatres of war like the Battle of the Somme were comparable. The shared sense of loss that people felt when one of these players fell provided a focus for the grief of a nation whose husbands, fathers, sons and brothers were being snatched away by the brutal conflict.

There is no shortage of incredible stories about these footballer-soldiers. Many went on to win decorations for bravery; a number won the Victoria Cross, and others the Distinguished Service Order, the Military Cross, the Distinguished Conduct Medal and the Military Medal. Some were commissioned as officers from the ranks, a rare privilege considering that most of them came from working-class and lower-middle-class backgrounds.

They fought and died in some of the most horrific battles of the First World War. Many of them even did so alongside each other, through the formation of footballing 'pals' battalions such as the 17th Battalion Middlesex Regiment and the 16th Battalion Royal Scots. There is camaraderie in playing for a football team, or in supporting one; it was a sad but necessary feature of the time that this camaraderie had to shift from the playing fields of the nation's football clubs to the killing fields of Verdun, Passchendaele and Ypres.

So while this book inevitably deals, at least in part, with the waging of war and the events of great battles, it is really a celebration of the men who, in peacetime, entertained enthusiastic crowds every Saturday on pitches up and down the country. Those games were a routine, a highlight of the week for fans and players alike – part of the British way of life. And it was to protect that way of life that these men hung up their boots and set out to the battlefields of Europe, many of them never to return.

I hope that this book helps us all to reflect upon the sacrifices they made.

Gary Lineker, 2014

1

The Lamps Go Out
Over Europe

The beginning of August 1914 was beautiful. Long hot days under cloudless skies were matched by warm summer evenings. Gorse flowers blazed like solar flares upon the hillsides, roses bloomed in the gardens of Britain, while poppies, brilliant red, littered the cornfields, blissfully free of the significance they would soon come to assume.

The first day of August that year was a Saturday, and what's more it was the beginning of a bank holiday weekend. As with bank holidays today when the sun is shining and the air is warm, people flocked to the seaside. Mixed bathing had only just been introduced and this revolutionary development doubtless added further excitement to the festive atmosphere at resorts up and down the country. Even the presence of self-appointed vigilantes – on the lookout for anyone whom they could report to the watch committee for showing too much flesh or being over-familiar with members of the opposite sex – failed to put a dampener on proceedings.

Out in the bays, paddle steamers threshed their way through the waters, their decks full of sightseers in brightly striped jackets and pale summer dresses. Further out, the white sails of yachts struggled to catch a breeze in the balmy weather.

People were happy.

For the majority of British people, the murder of Archduke Franz Ferdinand and his wife Sophie in Sarajevo on 28 June 1914 didn't seem particularly significant. Perhaps it might have merited a passing comment at the breakfast table before moving on to domestic matters; nothing more than that. The 'German Menace', which had been talked about for almost twenty years, seemed no more immediate on that day than on any other; while issues such as German naval expansion and pan-Slav agitation might bother the chattering classes, they were considered of little importance by the average person.

Members of the elite, however, had been aware which way the wind was blowing for some time. During Speech Day at Wellington College in 1909, former Prime Minister Lord Rosebery stated that 'the stress that patriotism will have to bear in days not far distant, and perhaps imminent, will be greater than has yet been known in the history of this country.' In 1910, following a holiday in France, the headmaster of New Beacon School in Sevenoaks told his pupils to prepare for war. And writing in 1911, Winston Churchill was preoccupied with 'the perils of war'.

Tension had been simmering for years between the great powers – Britain, Germany, France, Russia, Italy and Austria-Hungary – due to European colonial issues. This was then superseded by the problem of territorial rights in the Balkans. Alliances began to form between the nations: France, Britain and Russia formed the Triple Entente, while Germany, Austria-Hungary and Italy formed the Triple Alliance.

The assassination of the archduke burst a dam of international pressure. It precipitated Austria-Hungary's declaration of war on Serbia; on 28 July the first shots were fired. The conflict rapidly escalated as the countries of the Alliance and the Entente, bound by a series of interconnected treaties, involved themselves and declared war upon one another. Russia began to mobilise. Using their long-developed Schlieffen Plan, Germany moved to support the Austro-Hungarians and invaded neutral Belgium and Luxembourg before moving towards France. As a result of this, on 4 August 1914, just after that blissfully hot bank holiday, Britain declared war on Germany – honouring its promise to defend Belgian neutrality.

The conflict that would eventually come to be known as the First World War had begun. In the words of the British foreign secretary of the time, Sir Edward Grey: 'The lamps are going out all over Europe, we shall not see them lit again in our lifetime.'

Millions would die.

But on that August bank holiday weekend, the thoughts of most of Britain were focused not on impending hardships, but on leisure and relaxation. Both playing and following sport were of course favourite pastimes for many people, and football was rapidly becoming *the* sport. In 1914 both players and supporters must have been looking back in amazement at the changes that had occurred in the national game.

The organisation of the sport was perhaps the most unified it had ever been, with the Football Association having assumed near total control of the way it was run. This was by no means something that had happened overnight; the FA had been founded half a century previously on 26 October 1863, at the instigation of a London solicitor named Ebenezer Morley, who had also formed Barnes Football Club in 1862. In the mid nineteenth century, football was an entirely amateur affair and, like most sports, was played largely by well-off men and boys, many educated at public schools. This was something that would change radically in the decades which followed.

Representatives of a dozen clubs, mainly from London, were present at the meeting that agreed the formation of the FA. With no central governing body of any sort in existence prior to this point, many different versions of the game were being played. The primary object of the FA therefore became the establishment of a definite code of rules to regulate play and impose some kind of uniform standard upon the sport.

It is strange for us to imagine now, but at the subsequent meetings in which these rules were thrashed out, the general consensus was that football was a game that involved both the dribbling and the handling of the ball by players – it was perfectly permissible to make 'a fair catch'. Some more savage practices were also debated, such as 'hacking' – deliberately kicking another player in the leg. Astonishingly, some clubs at the time, including Blackheath, fought to retain this as a legal move, though it was eventually ruled out.

However, when the FA published its Laws of the Game it didn't mean for an immediate transformation in the way that the clubs across Britain played. Quite the contrary – clubs that did not wish to abide by these new rules could simply ignore them. It was another move, some years later, that really helped to widen the FA's sphere of influence.

In July 1871, a man called Charles Alcock, who had been serving as FA secretary for a year, came up with the idea of running a national knockout tournament. This became known as the Football Association Challenge Cup. Although the inaugural competition in 1871–72 was entered by only fifteen teams, the cup quickly became a focal point for the enthusiasm of fans. Smaller regional footballing associations began to spring up, and these in turn set up their own district and county cups. People's enjoyment of football was beginning to take place within an official structure.

It was also arguably the establishment of such competitions that led to the professionalisation of the game. Clubs with their eye on winning a coveted title began to feel that there was nothing wrong in paying for dedicated skilled players. This was especially true in the north, where football was becoming more the sport of working men – as opposed to the south, where many players were still public school 'old boys'.

Over the next few years the unsanctioned practice of paying players continued to spread, in spite of the complaints of the southern clubs. Eventually, in July 1885 the FA was forced to legalise professionalism in the game. This was a controversial move and many of the die-hard believers in football as an amateur pastime resented it for years to come, even as the sport continued to grow in popularity.

It is easy to see why club owners with a little business acumen might see advantages to professionalism. Salaried players with time to hone their skills would ensure a thrilling match for the fans to watch, hopefully topping it off with a win. Success kept the punters coming back, and if the punters kept coming back, so did their money – it may have been a little cynical, but it was also good sense. And the sums of money in question were rapidly increasing; in 1874 Aston Villa collected five shillings and two pence from gate receipts. Thirty years later, in 1904, they took £14,329 for a single match. Thousands of working-class men became deeply committed to their teams, going so far as to hold money back from the housekeeping to buy their tickets on Saturday afternoon. Montague Sherman wrote of this phenomenon in 1888:

No words of ours can adequately describe the present popularity of football with the public – a popularity which, though great in the metropolis, is infinitely greater in the large provincial towns.

The passion of the fans for their favourite players was intense and it is to this era that we can trace the emergence of the first true footballing superstars. Football cards bearing their images were sold in the thousands and they were approached on the streets by fans seeking their autographs. In some cases they received admiring letters from women suggesting marriage, or perhaps – scandalously for the time – a secret liaison. Of course the clubs were keen to encourage such adulation, as there would then be an even greater draw for the crowds.

The number of professional players in the game continued to grow rapidly. In 1891 the league had 448 registered players, most of whom were either full- or part-time professionals. By the outbreak of war in 1914 the Players' Union had a total of 4,470 professional players on their books. At the top end they could be earning as much as £4 a week, with star players earning considerably more through additional under-the-table payments.

However, throughout this period the tensions over professionalism continued to simmer, coming to a head in 1907 with the formation of the AFA, the Amateur Football Association, which was set up in opposition to the perceived 'corruption' of the game. Those that chose to become a part of the AFA (mainly clubs from London and the south-east) were forbidden to play against clubs who belonged to the FA – meaning, of course, that they could not compete for the FA Cup. However, although this bipartite system endured for some years, it became evident to all concerned that really such a division was in nobody's interests. In January 1914 the rift was healed and the AFA fell into line, becoming an FA-affiliated organisation.

By August 1914 the FA had imposed uniformity and coherence on the game, ending, to a large extent, the problem of rules and regulations that differed from region to region. An agreed code of conduct now bound all players, both amateur and professional. But if the world of football was at last feeling stable and united, this was in stark contrast to the condition of the wider world. Europe was at war.

At the time of the declaration of hostilities, the British army numbered about 250,000 troops stationed throughout the Empire. Added to this number were the reservists – a mixture of part-time soldiers who had undergone serious training and former soldiers who had already experienced war. These reservists were soon called up, swelling the total number of men available to the British high command to just over 700,000.

This was, of course, a vast number of troops. However, it paled in comparison to the might of the German war machine that – regular troops and reservists combined – numbered almost four million and was widely considered to be the best fighting force in the world. The German leader Kaiser Wilhelm notoriously dismissed the British Expeditionary Force (the name given to the army departing for the continent) as 'that contemptible little army'. Of course, Britain would not be facing Germany alone and its major ally, France, had an army of comparable size to that of Germany. In 1914 Britain was, in fact, the only major power involved in the conflict not to use some form of conscription in order to maintain its armed forces – compulsory military service was felt to be in opposition to British liberal traditions. In France, by comparison, as many as 80 per cent of men of military age were conscripted.

Lord Kitchener, Britain's newly appointed secretary of state for war, knew that yet more troops would be needed. While the majority of Britons were happy to believe the cheerfully patriotic idea that the war would be 'over by Christmas', Kitchener knew that in reality it was likely to be a protracted conflict. He therefore immediately began a massive voluntary recruitment drive, which would give birth to one of the most iconic images associated with the war.

With recruitment one of the major topics of the day, *London Opinion*, a popular weekly magazine, commissioned an artist called Alfred Leete to create an image for its cover. He duly did so and on 5 September 1914 the magazine was published bearing a now-famous image of Kitchener, formidable in military uniform and moustache, pointing directly out of the picture towards the viewer. Beside him were the words 'Your Country Needs You'.

The War Office immediately saw the potential of such an arresting image. Within a few hours of the magazine being published, they had purchased the rights to the picture and soon produced a poster of it, which became a ubiquitous sight all over the country. So much so that months later, on 3 January 1915, *The Times* wrote: 'Posters appealing to recruits are to be seen on every hoarding, in most windows, in omnibuses, tramcars and commercial vans. The great base of Nelson's Column is covered with them…Everywhere Lord Kitchener sternly points a monstrously big finger.'

The posters certainly influenced recruitment. In the first weeks of the war 33,000 men a week were joining up, but by the middle of September 1914 over half a million men had volunteered. It was an extraordinary number and a huge success for Kitchener. This was the birth of the 'New Army' or, as many called it, 'Kitchener's Army'.

Long queues could be seen outside recruiting offices from early in the morning until they closed at night. Some men even camped outside, determined to be the first to enlist the following morning. Recruiting staff worked sixteen hours a day, sleeping on the floor or under their desks. It was not unusual for a man's family to queue with him in order to be part of this patriotic endeavour; or else as the hours ticked by, wives and mothers would bring food and drink as their men patiently waited their turn.

There was a great sense of camaraderie; while men

enlisted for a variety of reasons, including patriotism and a sense of justice, for a lot of them one of the deciding factors in joining up seems to have been 'I went with my mate'.

Take Private J. Harwood, who joined the 6th Battalion Royal Berkshire Regiment:

> I worked for the County Council and, one morning, I left home to go to work; we were repairing the roads in Windsor Park at the time, but on the way I met a friend who was going to enlist. Instead of going on to work, I went back home, changed into my best clothes and went with him to the Recruiting Office at Reading.

Even boys so young as to be ineligible for service found ways of joining up, such as Charles Barff:

> I had run away from home when I was fifteen and joined up in Birmingham. I was very worried about my surname; I thought it sounded German. Anyway I didn't want my family to find me as I was only fifteen. I told the sergeant I was nearly twenty and gave a false name. My first name was Charles and I had a pal whose surname was Dickens. I thought

Charles Dickens sounded quite decent and I served under that name for two years.

This keenness to serve on the part of the country's young men was something that the upper echelons were naturally anxious to foster. It was General Sir Henry Rawlinson who suggested that men would be more likely to join the colours if being able to serve alongside one's friends became a formal arrangement. He then asked London stockbrokers to raise a battalion composed of City of London workers in order to set an example, which they duly did in late August 1914. This battalion, the 10th (Service) Battalion Royal Fusiliers quickly gained the nickname 'The Stockbrokers' Battalion'. Shortly after this, Lord Derby decided to try the same thing in Liverpool. Speaking to the volunteers he successfully recruited he said, 'This should be a battalion of pals, a battalion in which friends from the same office will fight shoulder to shoulder for the honour of Britain and the credit of Liverpool.'

These were the first of what became known as the 'pals battalions' and, seeing their success, Lord Kitchener encouraged similar recruiting endeavours across the country. Most of these were formed as local battalions drawing on specific cities, towns or regions but others, like the Stockbrokers' Battalion, were associated with a particular trade or occupation. Soon there were even battalions of sportsmen, but not footballers – not at first.

The cry for able young men had gone out, and the initial response of the nation had been strong. And yet, for all that they represented some of the nation's fittest young men, there were few professional footballers amongst those initial recruits. The reason for this was pretty straightforward: in August the FA secretary, Frederick Wall, had taken the decision that the forthcoming football season would continue as planned. He did so in spite of questions from certain quarters as to whether this was really appropriate when the nation was at war. The decision was made more controversial when other sports, such as cricket and rugby, quickly suspended their competitions.

Wall argued that the sport should continue in order to provide a pastime for those who were not undergoing military training, and so the matches continued. For professional players this presented a genuine obstacle to volunteering for service; most of them were under one-year renewable contracts, meaning that they could only enlist if their club agreed to release them.

However, given the heroic status that many players

enjoyed and the influence they had with the fans, it soon started to be felt by some that the lack of involvement of professional footballers in the war effort was far from a good thing. On 6 September 1914, no less a man than the creator of Sherlock Holmes, Sir Arthur Conan Doyle, appealed to footballers to hang up their boots for the duration of the conflict and join up:

> There was a time for all things in the world. There was a time for games, there was a time for business, there was a time for domestic life. There was a time for everything, but there is only time for one thing now, and that thing is war…If a footballer had strength of limb let them serve and march in the field of battle.

And the novelist Edward Phillips Oppenheim, author of *The Great Impersonation*, penned a few words for the *Daily Express*:

> For you who play football while others seek fame
> The knickers of sport are the garments of shame

But even in the face of such criticism the FA chose to press on with plans for the FA Cup. In fairness, they did so having consulted the War Office on the matter. On 8 September, Wall asked for an official sanction to continue with the season and made it clear that if the War Office felt this would be detrimental to the execution of the conflict then the FA would be fully prepared to request a general cessation of play. The reply came that: 'The question of whether the playing of matches should be stopped entirely is more a matter for the discretion of the Association, but the Council quite realise the difficulties involved in taking such an extreme step and they would deprecate anything being done which does not appear to be called for by the present situation.' As far as the army was concerned, for the present time football could continue.

In spite of the FA having sought official consultation, aggression towards football continued to grow. Such a swell of negative feeling was perhaps understandable; even only a few weeks into the war, it was already becoming clear that an easy victory was not on the cards. Indeed, things were not going well for the BEF (British Expeditionary Force) out in Europe.

During the first weeks of the war, German forces had advanced rapidly across France and come perilously close to Paris, only driven off thanks to an Allied victory at the First Battle of the Marne during the first half of September. Following this, both armies tried to outflank each other by moving northwards in a series of manoeuvres that became known as 'The Race to the Sea'. Neither side succeeded in gaining the advantage they sought.

The BEF then redeployed around the Belgian town of Ypres and began to advance eastwards, once again hoping to flank enemy forces. However, they soon ran into a mass of German forces who were themselves advancing with the objective of securing the ports on the Belgian coast. From 19 October to 22 November the two armies contended against each other in the series of bloody confrontations we know today as the First Battle of Ypres. On more than one occasion it seemed that the Germans would succeed in breaching the British lines; in the end they failed to do so, but the cost in British lives was extreme – casualties numbered more than 55,000.

With the stakes in Europe raised ever higher, it is not difficult to understand the perspective of those who railed against professional football. However, negative feelings directed towards the footballers themselves were not strictly fair – they continued to play to busy stadiums and, as far as they were aware, did so with the approval of the War Office. More than this, their contracts meant that without the agreement of their clubs and managers they were not able to stop playing even if they wanted to.

It would be wrong to think that the FA was actively attempting to obstruct recruitment in general – far from it. On 4 September all FA-affiliated clubs had been sent posters to display around their grounds. These proclaimed: 'Recruits for the Army are at the moment most urgently needed. Players and spectators who are physically fit and otherwise able are urged to join the Army at once.' This call was perhaps not met with a stampede of professional players eager to terminate their contracts, but individual clubs were also taking other steps to show willing – several, including Brighton & Hove Albion and Clapton Orient, instigated drilling practices for their teams.

It should also be remembered that there were professional players who did enlist at this time, in spite of the obstacles in their way. Donald Simpson Bell, known to his friends as Don or Donny, was one such player. Born in Harrogate on 3 December 1890, he was twenty-three when war broke out. He was also relatively unusual for a professional player at the time, in that he came from a middle-class family and had been lucky enough to receive a good education – he had won a scholarship to Knaresborough Grammar School and subsequently moved up to Westminster College. He cut an impressive figure: by the time he was sixteen he was over six foot tall and weighed more than fourteen stone. He was also a natural sportsman, captaining the athletics team and winning his colours for rugby, cricket, hockey, swimming and, of course, football.

Upon leaving school he decided to become a teacher and was appointed assistant master at Starbeck Council School near Harrogate, teaching English. He continued to be a keen footballer, turning out as an amateur for Crystal Palace and later Newcastle United. The latter club was doing particularly well at the time, having won the league on three occasions and taken part in five of the seven most recent FA Cup finals. Bell clearly remained a good all-rounder since he was also offered a county rugby cap for Herefordshire.

However, Bell soon began to find his modest schoolmaster's salary insufficient to meet his needs. He settled on the idea of playing football semi-professionally to supplement his pay, and signed with Bradford (in 1970, the club would become known Bradford Park Avenue, to avoid confusion with Bradford City). Bell made his Bradford debut against Wolverhampton Wanderers on 13 April 1913. He seems to have joined at a good time for the club because by 1914, Bradford had finally been promoted to the first division.

During the 1914–15 season Bell played in five matches but, bowing to the growing feeling that there were better ways for athletic young men to spend their time while the nation was at war, he asked to be released from his contract in order to join up. This request was granted and on 24 October 1914 Bell joined the ranks of the 6th Battalion West Yorkshire Regiment. In doing so he became one of the first professional footballers to enlist into the British army during the First World War. We will return to Bell later in this book to hear of his tremendous courage on the battlefield.

Spurs player Alexander McGregor is also notable for being a footballing first in the war, but a tragic one. He had joined up immediately upon declaration of war, becoming a private in the 1st Battalion Gordon Highlanders. However, on 14 December 1914, having only arrived at the front a few days previously, his letters home ceased. He had been killed in action.

Later, on 16 March 1915, the *Glasgow Herald* wrote of him:

Mrs. McGregor, 29 Cowlairs Avenue, Springburn, has received no word from her son, Private Alex.

McGregor, of the 1st Gordon Highlanders, since December 14. Private McGregor is well known as a football player, having played at centre-forward for Yoker Athletic last season. He subsequently signed for Tottenham Hotspur, to whom he went in August last. He, however, returned to Scotland, and enlisted in the Gordon Highlanders in November. After a stay in Aberdeen he left for the front on December 3.

McGregor is commemorated on panel 38 of the Ypres (Menin Gate) Memorial. He was the first foot-baller to fall in the war.

He would not be the last.

2

Football Pals

On 15 November 1914 a letter was published in the *Athletic News*. It was from Harold Tennant, the Under-Secretary of State for War, in reply to a letter from Tom Forsyth, the chairman of Airdrieonians. The Scottish Football Association, to which Airdrieonians belonged, had continued as normal, assured that the War Office had sanctioned this. However, in the face of mounting public criticism, Forsyth had written to Tennant asking him to clarify that this was indeed still the case. Tennant's reply was quite different to the previous line taken:

No objection is taken by the military authorities to occasional recreation. It is considered, however, that professional football does not come within that category, and that it can only be admitted on grounds of contract or employment. It is much more desirable that professional footballers should find employment in His Majesty's Forces than in their old occupation. With regard to the question of breach of contract, it is considered that this is a time when all should be prepared to make sacrifices.

This was a serious and unexpected blow to professional football; until this point the FA and SFA were secure in the fact that, whatever the opinion might be in certain quarters, they had a watertight moral defence for their decision to continue play – that they did so with War Office approval. With the publication of Tennant's comments, that defence had effectively vanished. It was, in modern terms, a public relations disaster.

Representatives of the English, Scottish, Welsh and Irish footballing ruling bodies swiftly convened for an emergency meeting. Seeking to shore up the damage, the FA issued vigorous appeals to its members, asking them to 'enlist today to show you are good sportsmen'. FA Secretary Frederick Wall also announced that 'special recruiting measures' would be taken at all matches across Britain the following weekend. So it was that on

Saturday 21 November, during half-time at matches up and down the nation, prominent men rose to their feet in order to address the crowds.

The sight that greeted these men, many of whom had never attended a football match before, probably surprised them a good deal. They had come prepared to exhort hundreds of shirking young men into doing their duty. But the make-up of the crowds at many of the grounds hardly fitted this image. There were a great many old men and, more importantly, there were a great many young men already clad in khaki. Most shocking of all, there were convalescing wounded soldiers in evidence! The total number of attendees was far smaller than they had been led to believe, and those that bothered to ask would have discovered that this was largely due to the fact that many men were either working extra shifts in factories or else had already enlisted and were undergoing training. Nevertheless, these public figures had come for a purpose and they duly delivered the rousing speeches they had prepared.

The results were considerably beneath expectations, with a mere handful of recruits being gathered as a result. A Cardiff City versus Bristol Rovers match saw six men enlist, and just one volunteered at Arsenal. In some places, such as Birmingham and

Nottingham Forest, the drive failed to secure even a single recruit. While the diminished numbers in the stands and the fact that many of those in attendance were apparently already soldiers might be mitigating factors, this still reflected incredibly badly on the institution of football and *The Times* ran the damning headline 'ONE RECRUIT AT ARSENAL MATCH'. Far from improving the public image of the game, the recruitment drive was spun so that football players and their fans appeared unpatriotic obsessives, valuing their beloved game over and above the safety of the nation. The situation was debated in the House of Commons, with MPs suggesting measures to curb attendance of matches – for example taxing all spectators who were not in military uniform. No such measures were ever instituted but it was a sign that antipathy towards professional football had reached a level at which the FA's position was becoming untenable.

There was arguably a considerable amount of hypocrisy in the way that so many people criticised the game; the hostility seems to have sprung at least partly from the reputation of football as the game of the working man. Horse racing was also still going on in spite of the war, but as a gentleman's sport it was not subjected to the same scathing public attacks.

The FA Council struck back in *The Times* on 27 November, publishing a well-reasoned rebuttal of the accusations levelled against the game. In it, they claimed that more than 100,000 recruits had come from Association Football and that this was more than the number of enlistees from all other branches of sport. They went on to point out that, as for the matter of the players themselves, there were fewer than 5,000 professionals in the whole country, 2,000 of whom were already serving in the military in some capacity. Against the estimated two million unmarried men of military age nationwide who had yet to enlist, the attack on football seemed entirely disproportionate. Finally, they drew attention to the fact that clubs were bound to pay their players their agreed rates; they could not simply cancel their contracts. If, on the other hand, players wished to leave they could ask that their contract be terminated. Not a single player who had made this request had been refused.

While these were all perfectly sensible points they did very little to silence football's critics – in England, at least, the furore continued. Even members of the clergy became involved; while on a pastoral visit to Bethnal Green the Bishop of Chelmsford, the Right Reverend John Watts-Ditchfield, gave a sermon in favour of footballers leaving their teams to join the forces. His words were summarised in the 2 December edition of the *Stratford Express*:

> He felt that the cry against professional football at the present time was right. He could not understand men who had any feeling, any respect for their country, men in the prime of life, taking large salaries at a time like this for kicking a ball about. It seemed to him something incongruous and unworthy.

North of the border, in Scotland, things played out somewhat differently. At the time, Heart of Midlothian were top of the Scottish First Division, having enjoyed eight straight victories, including a 2-0 win against the previous champions, Celtic. Scottish players were receiving the same kind of criticism in the press as their English counterparts, and given their high-flying status it was natural enough that the debate would come to involve the Hearts team. On 16 November, one 'Soldier's Daughter' had written a stinging rebuke that was published in the *Evening News*: 'While Hearts continue to play football, enabled thus to pursue their peaceful play by the sacrifice of the lives of thousands of their countrymen, they might adopt, temporarily, a

nom de plume, say, The White Feathers of Midlothian.'
This reference to white feathers, a traditional symbol
of cowardice, cannot have been received well by either
the players or the administration at Hearts.

Coincidentally, almost immediately after this letter
appeared, Sir George McCrae, a well-known textile
merchant and the former MP for Edinburgh East, made
a momentous decision. On Thursday 19 November
the *Evening Dispatch* informed its readership that Sir
George had volunteered for service. In fact the paper
didn't quite have the full story; the following morning
The Scotsman explained that McCrae had approached
the War Office and offered to raise and command a battalion of local men for service in France. That same day,
125 George Street, where McCrae lived, was besieged
by hundreds of young men eager to do their bit and at
4 p.m. McCrae himself appeared to loud applause and
cheers. Once he had managed to quiet the excitable
crowd he announced that recruitment for his battalion, the 16th Royal Scots, would formally commence
on Friday 27 November with a large public meeting in
the Usher Hall. He told the assembly that he expected
to fill the ranks within seven days. Some people seriously doubted that this could be done, but Sir George
was adamant: seven days.

It was the perfect opportunity for the Hearts players to prove their mettle and they seized it with both hands. By the official recruitment date, sixteen players from the club had already agreed to join the battalion. As an aside, it is surprising to note that of this sixteen, five were turned away on the grounds of ill health; problems ranged from asthma to tuberculosis to a weak heart. For professional athletes to suffer such problems perhaps gives us an insight into the state of health among the general working populace at the time.

There were plenty of notable players among the volunteers. One was Duncan Currie, born on 13 August 1892 in Kilwinning, Ayrshire, the son of a foundry patternmaker. Football seems to have been in his blood: his father was a goalkeeper and his brothers both played – Robert for Hearts and for Bury, and Sam for Leicester Fosse. Duncan first played for Kilwinning Rangers before being transferred to Heart of Midlothian for the grand sum of £2. Both strong and quick, he was a valued centre-half who could also play at left-back.

Tom Gracie pledged his service at the same time as Duncan Currie. He was slightly younger, having been born on 12 June 1889 in Yorkhill, Glasgow. On leaving school he studied bookkeeping and went on to work as a meat salesman. He played for both Shawfield and Strathclyde before joining his first league side, Airdrieonians, in 1907. He kept moving around, spending short spells at both Hamilton Academical and Arthurlie, and then signed for Morton in 1909. In 1911 he was selected to play for Scotland in their match against England at Goodison Park. However, he was kept on the bench for the entire game and was never selected to play for his country again.

It wasn't all bad news for Tom, though, as on the very same day he signed with Everton. He remained there for a season but, never one to stay put if he didn't have to, went to their arch-rivals Liverpool. Unfortunately he didn't do particularly well there and played only occasionally during his two-and-a-half seasons with the club. He returned to Scotland the very year war broke out, joining Hearts for £400 as a replacement for Percy Dawson, who had moved to Blackburn for a then record transfer fee of £2,500. Things went better for Tom north of the border and during the 1914–15 season he was the Scottish Football League's joint top scorer (sharing the honour with James Richardson of Ayr United), and got one of the crucial goals in Hearts' 2-0 defeat of Celtic, securing their position as the new Scottish champions.

Henry Wattie, born in Edinburgh on 2 June 1893,

was also one of the first to sign up. The son of a coachman and the youngest of five brothers, he played for several junior teams, including Tranent, and became a Hearts player in 1913. He was an inside forward to be feared, scoring against even the toughest opposition – in his debut match for Hearts he put in two goals against the mighty Rangers at Ibrox, securing a 2-1 victory. He was as tough as they come, as two Aberdeen defenders once discovered to their cost when trying to tackle him – one was injured badly enough that he couldn't play on after half-time, while the other suffered a broken leg!

With such sporting heroes pledging their service it is not surprising that a buzz began to grow around McCrae's battalion. After the news about the players joining up became public, McCrae received telegrams from such luminaries as Lord Kitchener, Winston Churchill, David Lloyd George and the prime minister, Herbert Asquith.

Momentum began to build, and that evening a couple more players, Pat Crossan and Jim Boyd, threw their hats in the ring and said they would enlist too. Crossan was a player worthy of note. He was the same age as Wattie and the two were great friends. In fact their connection went further – Wattie's sister Alice was engaged to Crossan. As a player Crossan was renowned for two things. The first was his incredible speed – he supplemented his income by racing professionally as a sprinter. The second was his (somewhat affected) vanity. Crossan thought himself very handsome and said that any female fans of Hearts were probably there solely because of him. His teammates enjoyed joking about this absurd attitude and Wattie once said: 'Pat can maybe pass the ball, but he couldn't pass a mirror if he tried.'

On Friday 27 November the meeting at the Usher Hall to officially begin recruitment took place as planned. As might have been predicted by this point, it was a roaring success. An estimated 4,000 people were gathered outside the doors by the time they opened at 7.30 p.m. and the auditorium was unable contain the crush. The Hearts players who had already pledged their service were visible on the stage along with various other important people, including Sir George McCrae himself. When the time came for him to speak he rose to his feet to thunderous applause. Someone at the back shouted 'Well done, Sir George!', to which he replied:

This is not a night for titles. I stand before you humbly as a fellow Scot. Nothing more and nothing less. You know I don't speak easily of crisis, but that is what confronts us. I have received permission from the War Office to raise a new battalion for active service. It is my intention that this unit will reflect accurately all the many classes of this famous capital, and that it will be characterised by such a spirit of excellence that the rest of Lord Kitchener's Army will be judged by our standard. Furthermore, with the agreement of the authorities, I have undertaken to lead the battalion in the field. I would not – I could not – ask you to serve unless I share the danger at your side. In a moment I will walk down to Castle Street and set my name to the list of volunteers. Who will join me?

That is exactly what he did, and men followed in their droves. By midnight almost 300 men had enlisted, and over the coming days the ranks continued to swell. Inspired by the example of the players, an estimated 500 Hearts supporters eventually joined up, along with 150 Hibernian supporters and players, and a number of professional players from other clubs such as Raith Rovers, Dunfermline and Falkirk. There could be no clearer example of the enormous influence the players had on their fans, and the effect that this could have on recruitment efforts. The 16th Royal Scots, or 'The Sportsmen's Battalion' as they came to be known, could for ever lay claim to being the first footballing pals battalion.

Shortly afterwards, the *People's Journal* published sheet music for a song about Heart of Midlothian, written by T. M. Davidson with music by David Stephen:

Hearts Lead the Way

When the Empire is in danger, and we hear our country's call,
The Mother-land may count on us to leave the leather ball.
We've hacked our way in many a fray, we've passed and gone
   for goal,
But a bigger field awaits us, and we were keen to join the roll.

So it's right wing, left wing, front line and goal;
Half back, full back, every living soul;
Sound o' wind, strong of limb, eager for the fray,
Every soul for the goal Hearts! Hearts! Hearts lead the way!

We thank the Lord Almighty He has made us strong and fit,
Our muscles are like iron and we don't know when we're hit.
We take a lot of mauling, we can give as good's we get,
And we wish to show the Germans we are not decadent yet.

So it's right wing, left wing, front line and goal;
Half back, full back, every living soul;
Sound o' wind, strong of limb, eager for the fray,
Every soul for the goal Hearts! Hearts! Hearts lead the way!

Grandstand, pavilion, friend or foe, we bid you all adieu,
We know your thoughts are with us when we go to fight for you.
You've seen us win, you've seen us lose, but now we join the fray
Where brute and bully must go down, and honour win the day.

So it's right wing, left wing, front line and goal;
Half back, full back, every living soul;
Sound o' wind, strong of limb, eager for the fray,
Every soul for the goal Hearts! Hearts! Hearts lead the way!

The tremendous success of McCrae's efforts made no small impression south of the border. Although recruiting football fans during actual matches had proved something of a failure, some began to think that the success of a footballing pals battalion could be replicated in England.

William Joynson-Hicks, popularly known as 'Jix', was a solicitor and the Unionist MP for Brentford. He had been an enthusiastic and energetic campaigner for the war effort from the moment hostilities had been declared and had involved himself in various schemes and initiatives, sitting on several committees. A few days after the raising of McCrae's battalion he happened to be visiting the War Office on some unconnected matter. There, it was mentioned to him that if he was looking for further projects that would be beneficial to the cause, he might consider lending his talents to the raising of an English footballers' battalion.

Jix wasn't a man to rest on his laurels. He immediately made contact with the FA and on 5 December 1914 the association sent a letter to the secretaries of eleven professional clubs, inviting them to attend a meeting on 8 December. This came only two days after the four national Football Associations, still besieged by criticism, had agreed to suspend international matches – and being seen to make a more positive contribution to the war could only be a good thing. Joynson-Hicks chaired the meeting, which took place at the FA offices in Russell Square. The resolution that was eventually reached was straight to the point: 'That this meeting with the directors of London professional football clubs heartily favours the project of the formation of a Footballers' Battalion.' A committee to oversee the process was formed and all the professional football players in London, plus a considerable number from elsewhere in the country, were subsequently invited to a meeting on 15 December at Fulham Town Hall.

As with the meeting in Edinburgh, it was underestimated just how many players would attend; there were over 400 on the day, meaning that proceedings had to be moved to the largest public room within the town hall. Jix opened proceedings with a speech alluding to the seriousness of the war and the fact that the formation of this battalion was, in his opinion, the best way to answer professional football's critics. He was followed by William Hayes Fisher MP, the president of Fulham Football Club, who had arranged for the use of the hall. After him was Lord Kinnaird, president of the FA and a respected former player himself. Each in his own way exhorted, cajoled or reassured those present until, last of all, Captain Thomas Whiffen, London's chief recruiting officer, rose and appealed for volunteers to come forward.

The first player to do so was the captain of Clapton Orient, Fred 'Spider' Parker. After him came Archie Needham of Brighton & Hove Albion and then Frank Buckley. The latter already had military experience and had actually offered his services as soon as he heard about the plans for forming a battalion, a few days before. Others joined them, until in total 35 professional players had signed up, drawn from the ranks of Arsenal, Bradford City, Brighton & Hove Albion, Clapton Orient, Croydon Common, Crystal Palace, Luton Town, Southend United, Tottenham Hotspur and Watford.

The War Office had given permission for the unit to be officially known as the 17th (Service) Battalion Middlesex Regiment. The regiment had the nickname 'Die Hards', earned while fighting under the Duke of Wellington in the Peninsular War more than a century earlier. In the Battle of Albuera on 16 May 1811, the 57th Regiment of Foot (as they were then known), had stood against a far larger French force. Their commander, Colonel William Inglis, was badly wounded in the fighting and as he lay dying screamed at his men, 'Die hard, 57th! Die hard!'

But whatever name the battalion might have been given officially, for many it would come to be known simply as 'The Footballers' Battalion'.

In the days and weeks that followed the initial meeting, the command structures for the battalion were put in place. Two retired army officers, Colonel Charles Grantham and Colonel Henry Fenwick, became commanding officer and second in command respectively.

West Africa House on Kingsway was selected as the site for the first battalion parade, which was scheduled to take place in early January 1915. Certain regulations were relaxed for players who chose to join the battalion: in particular they were given leave from military training to continue to play for their clubs in league and cup matches for the remainder of the season.

Recruitment posters were designed and plastered in and around football stadiums. They read: 'The Footballers' Battalion wants players, officials, and club enthusiasts. Are YOU fit and free?' The second footballing pals battalion was under way.

3

A Brief Respite

By December 1914 it had become all too clear that the war wasn't going to be over quickly as everyone had hoped. Had people known just how protracted and bloody a conflict it was to be, they would have trembled. Following its opening campaigns, with each side attempting to outmanoeuvre the other, the war had now solidified into one of attrition. There was a continuous front line running from the North Sea to the Swiss frontier, occupied on both sides by armies in trenches and prepared defensive positions. It was stalemate, and with the worsening winter weather the armies would have to wait until spring 1915 for a fresh series of offensives.

Over the previous months the real impact of the war in terms of loss of life had become apparent. Casualties were mounting and the inevitable dreaded telegrams informing relatives of soldiers' deaths began to be delivered across Britain. Soon everyone knew, or had heard of, a family who had been touched by tragedy, even if they were lucky enough for this not to be the case with their own. Household names from the sporting world started to appear on the rolls of the fallen, for example Gerard 'Twiggy' Anderson, a fellow of All Souls College, Oxford, and the greatest hurdler of his time, who was killed on 9 November 1914 with the Cheshire Regiment. Of course the majority of professional footballers were, for the time being, safe from such a fate, as they had been later in enlisting. But there was an important football-related incident, and it is one that I simply cannot leave out of this book, despite the fact it is not a story about league players. I am talking, of course, about the Christmas Truce of 1914.

During the lead-up to Christmas there were a number of peace initiatives. One was the famous Open Christmas Letter, a public message of peace written and circulated by welfare campaigner Emily Hobhouse. The letter was addressed 'To the Women of Germany and Austria' and was signed by 101 of Britain's leading suffragists. It included the words: 'Is it not our mission to preserve life? Do not humanity and common sense alike prompt us to join hands with the women of neutral countries, and urge our rulers to stay further bloodshed?' The pope at the time, Benedict XV, also asked for a truce over Christmas, exhorting that 'the guns may fall silent at least upon the night the angels sang'. Yet these requests and others went unheeded by both sides: there would be no official ceasefire.

But Christmas as an annual holiday was extremely important to both the British and the Germans – probably the most important time of the year for either side. Both sides shared the same date for Christmas Day, 25 December, unlike the Russians who celebrated it some weeks later. In fact many British Christian traditions, Christmas trees for example, actually came from Germany and were introduced to Britain by Queen Victoria's consort, Prince Albert. The Christian beliefs that both armies shared, and the strong associations with hope and new beginnings that Christmas carried, probably played a large part in what happened at the end of 1914.

No serious military actions were planned over the Christmas period since the generals of both sides wished to allow their men in the trenches a brief respite to enjoy whatever meagre celebrations they might be able to – and they most likely also wanted to make merry themselves. So it was that the soldiers on both sides ended up enjoying their festivities just metres away from each other, huddled against the hard frost that had set in, separated only by the short distance of no man's land.

Although there was no official ceasefire, a series of unofficial ceasefires took place along the Western Front over the Christmas period in 1914. They started gently enough, as these things do. Soldiers began to shout Christmas greetings across to each other. Voices were raised in carols recognised by both sides. In some instances, as extraordinary as it may seem, men actually began to leave the trenches to meet each other in no man's land. A dangerous thing to do, to be sure, but it happened nevertheless. One Private Scrutton from the Essex Regiment describes such an occurrence in a letter that was published in the *Norfolk Chronicle* on 1 January 1915: 'One of our fellows thereupon stuffed his pocket with fags and got over the trench. The German got over his trench, and right enough they met half way and shook hands, Fritz taking the fags and giving cheese in exchange.'

Although we will never be sure of the exact number

of men involved, it is estimated that over 100,000 British and German troops took part in these unofficial cessations of hostilities. Aside from the exchange of simple gifts it seems that, in some locales at least, all kinds of unusual interactions took place as both sides became less wary of each other. The humorist and cartoonist Bruce Bairnsfather was serving with the Royal Warwickshire Regiment. He described his experiences in a letter home:

> I wouldn't have missed that unique and weird Christmas Day for anything . . . I spotted a German officer, some sort of lieutenant I should think, and being a bit of a collector, I intimated to him that I had taken a fancy to some of his buttons . . . I brought out my wire clippers and, with a few deft snips, removed a couple of his buttons and put them in my pocket. I then gave him two of mine in exchange . . . The last I saw was one of my machine gunners, who was a bit of an amateur hairdresser in civil life, cutting the unnaturally long hair of a docile Boche, who was patiently kneeling on the ground whilst the automatic clippers crept up the back of his neck.

There was another element to the interaction

between the armies that recurred up and down the lines: football. There are multiple reports of games between the British and German soldiers. One such account comes from a letter, published in *The Times* on 1 January 1915, from an anonymous major who claimed: 'The...regiment actually had a football match with the Saxons, who beat them 3-2.' We can assume the Germans won on penalties!

Casual games were apparently happening all along the Western Front. One of the best accounts is from Ernie Williams of the 6th Cheshire Regiment, who said later in an interview:

> The ball appeared from somewhere, I don't know where, but it came from their side – it wasn't from our side that the ball came. They made up some goals and one fellow went in goal and then it was just a general kickabout. I should think there were about a couple of hundred taking part. I had a go at the ball. I was pretty good then, at 19. Everybody seemed to be enjoying themselves. There was no sort of ill-will between us. There was no referee, and no score, no tally at all. It was simply a melee – nothing like the soccer you see on television. The boots we wore were a menace – those great big boots we had

on – and in those days the balls were made of leather
and they soon got very soggy.

It would be misleading to paint the events of Christmas 1914 as universally peaceful – eighty-one British soldiers died on Christmas Day, either victims of alert snipers in otherwise peaceful areas or in pockets where, for one reason or another, the fighting continued. Nevertheless, along great swathes of the Western Front the guns did fall silent for a day. It speaks volumes that in the awkward business of communicating across divisions of nationality and across battle lines, football was the common language that many turned to. It became a common denominator that drew the two sides together for a few hours of peace and humanity amid the horrors of war. This was the game at its very best.

When British high command heard of these informal truces they were extremely unhappy, and severe orders were issued regarding fraternisation with the enemy. In spite of this, it has been recorded that unsanctioned ceasefires took place in subsequent years. These were on a much smaller scale, however, and it is the truce of 1914 that has gone down as one of the few compassionate moments in one of the bloodiest wars in human history.

*

Following that brief lull both sides were gearing up for a year of combat that would redefine modern warfare. In January 1915 Germany deployed a terrifying new weapon against Britain. On the night of 19 January 1915, Zeppelin airships undertook a successful bombing raid on England, dropping bombs on Great Yarmouth, Sheringham and King's Lynn. When viewed against the horrifying casualty lists of the war as a whole, the four people killed and sixteen seriously injured in this raid do not seem like a vast number. But the German objective was as much to sow fear among the population – as Alfred von Tirpitz, Secretary of State of the German Imperial Naval Office, said: 'The measure of success will lie not only in the injury which will be caused to the enemy, but also in the significant effect it will have in diminishing the enemy's determination to prosecute the war.'

Certainly Britons could no longer feel that their island was a secure fortress. Even London was successfully targeted in May, with Stoke Newington and Stepney taking the brunt of what would be the first of many such attacks on the capital. In 1915 alone there were a total of twenty Zeppelin raids on Britain, killing 181 people and injuring another 455, as well as doing considerable damage to property. The authorities tried to turn these new and unpredictable attacks to their advantage: new recruiting posters were released bearing the words: 'It is far better to face the bullets than to be killed at home by a bomb.' Germany had changed the nature of the war with these aerial terror attacks, and it was about to do so again in a different way.

The Belgian town of Ypres remained a key strategic point, which the Allies had successfully held during the fierce fighting at the end of 1914. As the weather began to improve again in spring 1915, it was inevitable that the conflict there would intensify once more. But that the Germans would choose to deploy a weapon illegal under international law was something that nobody was expecting.

On 22 April 1915 the German army released 168 tons of chlorine gas just north of Ypres. Carried by a slight easterly breeze, a thick greenish-grey cloud crept across the battlefield to envelop positions held by French colonial troops from Martinique. Chlorine is an extreme irritant to the eyes, throat and lungs. Exposure to high concentrations can easily be fatal, causing death by asphyxiation. Unfortunately the officers in charge of the French troops suspected that the cloud was a cover for a German advance rather than a poison attack, and they told their men to 'stand to'. It did not take long for the terrible effects of the gas to be felt, and the French quickly broke ranks, abandoning their trenches to flee from the choking fumes.

As a result over four miles of the Allied line, a significant portion, was left undefended, and the Germans might easily have broken through. But the German soldiers were understandably wary of the gas themselves and so delayed their advance, giving the nearby 1st Canadian Division enough time to bravely rush in and seal the breach.

While the majority of footballers had still not entered the arena of war, there was one former league player who was nearby when this attack occurred (though he was not on the section of the line where the gas attack actually occurred). That man was Gerald Kirk.

Kirk was born on 14 July 1883 and, rather unusually for a footballer playing at the national level for a northern club, came from a privileged background – his family were landowners in Ingleton, Yorkshire. It was while he was attending Pocklington Grammar School as a boarder that his passion for football was ignited, in spite of the fact that the school placed a greater emphasis on rugby. Kirk went on to captain the local amateur side, Ingleton, and was part of the team that won the Lancaster and District League Championship in 1903.

On 25 April 1905 Gerald joined Bradford City in the Second Division, after impressing in a trial against Dundee and again in a trial against Blackburn Rovers. Despite being offered a contract, he remained an amateur. Kirk made his debut first-team appearance for the Bantams in a 2-0 victory over Blackpool at Valley Parade on 28 October 1905. He went on to become the club's established centre-half, making forty league appearances. In 1906 Kirk was transferred to Leeds City, for whom he played seven times before returning to Bradford City in September 1907. During the 1907–08 season he turned out only three times for the first team, spending most of his time in the reserves.

Disheartened, Kirk decided to retire from national football, though he was still only twenty-six years old. He didn't give football up altogether, however, and returned to his old amateur club, Ingleton. He married his sweetheart, Sarah Jane Capstick, on 21 April 1909 and settled into local life. He was active in the community, helping to establish the Ingleton Conservative Club and sitting on the board of Ingleton National School. It seemed he was content.

But on 1 September 1914 Gerald enlisted into the

ranks of the 1/5th Battalion Royal Lancaster Regiment. In spite of his social position – Kirk gave his profession as 'gentleman' – he did not push for a commission as an officer, as was often the case with men of his standing, and he became 'Private 2132'. The following October he was promoted to lance corporal. His battalion was initially involved with home defence duties, guarding the Great Western Railway line between Didcot and Oxford. In November they left Didcot for Sevenoaks in Kent, where they combined with troops from the Territorial West Lancashire Division. In January 1915 Gerald was commissioned as a second lieutenant and on 17 February 1915 the battalion finally sailed for France, landing at Le Havre. They had the distinction of being one of the first territorial units to be sent overseas.

By 12 April the battalion was serving near the town of Ypres, and had taken up position in the front-line trenches. Five days of fighting followed, with the unit suffering under heavy shellfire. In this time they lost fourteen men, with a further forty-four wounded. It was immediately after this that the German chlorine gas attack occurred. Gerald Kirk and his comrades were brought forward to support the 1st Canadian Division. On 23 April, the day after the gas attack, they were waiting in reserve when the Allied counter-attack began.

They were called upon at 5 p.m. The battalion immediately came under heavy rifle and machine-gun fire, and with little cover to aid their advance they were quickly cut to ribbons. Twenty-six of their number were killed and 102 were wounded. Kirk himself was hit in the chest by machine-gun fire while leading his men forward. Seriously wounded, he was taken to a first-aid station in the town of Poperinghe, a short distance behind the lines. There was nothing they could do to save him; he died the following day, on 24 April 1915. He is buried at Poperinghe Old Military Cemetery: plot 2, row K, grave 28. The German attack on Ypres had been blunted by the Allied retaliation, but at a great cost in life. Gerald Kirk was one such life – he would never enjoy a kick-about with his friends from Ingleton again.

To take part in an attack as Kirk did must have required tremendous courage and strength of will. And yet men were frequently required to walk into terrible danger in this way during the First World War. Such actions were what you might call 'ordinary heroics'. This is not to denigrate them in any way, but simply to acknowledge that in this conflict of conflicts they became the norm. This being the case, to be formally commended for one's actions in battle usually meant that some truly extraordinary deed had occurred. Certainly the actions of footballer William Angus in June 1915 qualified as such.

William Angus, known as Willie, was born on 28 February 1888 in Armadale, a small town in West Lothian, Scotland. On leaving school he began work as a miner, playing football as an amateur for the local team, Carluke Rovers. In 1911 he signed for Celtic, going on to turn out for the club during the 1912–13 and 1913–14 seasons. It was not, however, a distinguished stint, and he played for the first team on only one occasion. He was released from his contract and was captaining Wishaw Athletic by the time war broke out.

Soon after hostilities began, a recruiting drive was held near Carluke, during which Sergeant Major George Caven from the Highland Light Infantry impressed upon the young men of the town the need for more troops at the front. Willie Angus didn't hesitate – he signed up immediately. So did a man called James Martin. The two didn't know it, but their lives were to become inextricably linked by the war.

Angus and Martin, along with the rest of the volunteers, were sent to train with the Highland Light

Infantry but were subsequently told that their battalion was not going to be sent into action for some time. As a result of this both men transferred to the 8th Battalion Royal Scots, who were about to set out for the front. So it was that in June 1915, the two of them were in a front-line trench on the outskirts of Givenchy-lès-la-Bassée in northern France. Martin, who had an officer's commission, was serving as a lieutenant, while Angus held the more humble rank of lance corporal.

On their part of the line the trenches of the opposing forces were only about 70 yards apart. The Allies had managed to push the German line back some distance, except for round an elevated embankment known from map notation as 'Point 14'. Its height and the view of no man's land that it afforded gave the Germans a significant advantage and, as a result, it had proved impossible for the British troops to advance any further. Point 14 would have to be destroyed.

The decision was made to send a bombing party to take out the position. It was to be led by Lieutenant Martin, and would take place on the night of 11 June. Unfortunately the Germans were expecting such an attempt; as soon as the attack was launched they exploded a mine they had dug into the embankment, creating a crater fifteen feet wide and forcing the men of the 8th Royal Scots into a desperate retreat. It was only when they reached the relative safety of their own lines and took stock of the situation that they realised one of their number was missing: James Martin.

It wasn't until dawn began to suffuse the sky the next day that it became apparent what had happened. In the pale morning light, Martin's body was visible, lying out on the embankment close to the enemy machine guns. Even as his comrades watched he stirred feebly: he was still alive.

Alive he might have been, but it was clear that he was also grievously injured. If he was to have any hope of survival he would need to be given medical help as soon as possible, yet given how close he lay to the German lines it was hard to see how anything could be done.

The sun climbed higher in the sky and soon Martin was suffering in the heat of a bright summer day. He pleaded weakly with the Germans to let him have a drink of water. Their response was a bomb thrown over the parapet to try to finish him off. It failed to kill him, but the 8th Royal Scots were outraged. It was then that Willie Angus made an incredibly brave offer: he said that he would go out and try to bring Martin back. At first his offer was refused by the officer in charge.

However, Brigadier General Lawford arrived on the scene and gave his permission for the rescue attempt to continue. Given the severity of the situation, doubtless many thought that what Angus was doing was tantamount to suicide.

A rope was tied around Angus so that he could be dragged back to the British lines if he was wounded. This done, he climbed his way out of the trenches and crept across no man's land, using the natural cover on the ground to conceal himself. Miraculously he managed to reach Martin's side without being detected. Once there he removed the rope and tied it around Martin. He then gave the injured man a drink of brandy to prepare him for the ordeal they still had to face: a headlong race back across no man's land – in full view of the enemy.

While this was happening, the Germans realised that something was going on and began to throw more bombs out of their trenches towards the two men. It was now or never.

Angus managed to get Martin to his feet and started to carry him back towards safety. As he did so, an explosion of rifle and machine-gun fire from the Germans rent the air. Blasts from dozens more explosives went off all around them. However, in spite of the danger, in some ways the dust that these bombs created actually did more to protect Angus and Martin than harm them, since it stopped the enemy snipers getting a line on them.

Nevertheless, Angus was hit by several bullets and fell to the ground more than once. Incredibly, upon each occasion he somehow managed to get back up and continued to drag Martin towards the British trenches. He was already seriously wounded when he signalled to their comrades to pull Martin in using the safety rope.

Angus then carried out his most breathtakingly courageous act. As soon as the others started hauling Martin in, Angus began to move along the length of the trench, drawing the fire of the enemy so as to allow Martin to be brought to safety without further injury. The same could not be said of Angus, who was brought down several more times. When he finally collapsed into the British trench he was rushed to the medical station more dead than alive. He had been wounded no fewer than forty times.

Lieutenant Colonel Gemmill, the officer commanding at Givenchy, later wrote: 'No braver deed was ever done in the history of the British Army'. It is hard to disagree with that statement.

Against the odds both men survived, though Angus's injuries cost him his left eye and right foot, putting an end to his footballing career. He returned to Britain, and on 30 August 1915 King George V presented him with the Victoria Cross at Buckingham Palace, making him the first Scottish territorial soldier to receive such an honour.

On returning to Scotland he was feted by the whole footballing community and received standing ovations at both Celtic Park and Ibrox on the same day, where the two semi-finals of the Glasgow Cup were taking place. Both Angus and Martin eventually returned to Carluke, where they remained friends for the rest of their lives. On each anniversary of the event, Martin sent Angus a telegram that read simply: 'Congratulations on the 12th'. When Martin died in 1956 his brother continued this tradition. Angus himself passed away just a couple of days after the forty-fourth anniversary of his heroic deed, on 14 June 1959.

But in spite of the bravery and tenacity of men like Willie Angus, little really changed on the Western Front. The slow brutal war ground on, with neither side able to gain the decisive advantage they so desperately wanted.

4

On Further Shores

The Western Front was not, of course, the only place in which the war was being fought – one of the most notable campaigns of the conflict aside from the battles in Belgium and France had also got under way in 1915: the Gallipoli campaign.

The Gallipoli peninsula lay within the Ottoman Empire, in what is now Turkey, and formed the northern bank of the Dardanelles, a strait that ultimately connects the Black Sea to the Aegean Sea and thereby provides Russia with a sea route. Russia had allied itself with Britain and France in the war, while the Ottoman Empire had declared itself for the Central Powers (joining Germany, Austria-Hungary and Bulgaria). The

Ottoman Empire therefore closed the strait to Allied vessels and even mined it to prevent unwanted ships from gaining passage.

As a result, on 18 March France and Britain initiated a joint naval bombardment of the peninsula, with the objective of securing it before mounting an attack on Constantinople (modern Istanbul). Not only would a swift victory open the way for Russia's ships once more but, so the thinking went, it would open a new front against the Germans. Unfortunately the naval assault did not go well – three British destroyers were severely damaged in the exchange of fire with the Turks and a French battleship sank after hitting a mine. Almost 700 Allied lives were lost without any significant damage being done to the Ottoman defences. The assault was therefore abandoned; it would be 25 April before another attempt to secure the strait was made, this time by landing troops on the peninsula in order to capture the Turkish forts. However, in the five weeks since the initial attack the Turkish forces had been able to gather significant reinforcements. This did not bode well for the Allies.

Among the British personnel who were involved in the campaign was a man who was one of the true footballing superstars of the age, a goalkeeper known both for his idiosyncratic but highly effective style of play and his tremendous charisma: Leigh Roose.

Leigh Richmond Roose, often known as 'Dick', was born in the village of Holt on the Welsh border in 1877, the fourth son of Presbyterian minister Richmond Roose and his wife Eliza. Roose cannot have had an easy childhood; his mother passed away as a result of cancer when he was just four years old – she was only thirty-five at the time. As he grew older he was educated at Holt Academy before leaving home for Aberystwyth to study at the University of Wales. He quickly became something of a footballing legend on the campus team, and wasted no time taking advantage of the fact that he was no longer under the direct supervision of his father in order to develop what would become another life-long interest – flirting with girls. He was a handsome young man and these looks, combined with his prowess on the pitch, apparently drew female students to watch his matches in spite of there being rules against the sexes mingling at the ground.

Roose's talents were quickly recognised by the local amateur club Aberystwyth Town and he began to play for them during the 1898–99 season. Even at this early stage in his career Roose was developing a remarkable style of play. It was the norm for goalkeepers to stick very close to their goals, rarely venturing out of the box. Not so Roose, who would spend a considerable amount of time 'sweeping' – tidying up loose balls behind his defenders.

And it didn't stop there. One particular rule of the game that was in force at this time was Law 8. It quite clearly stated that 'the goalkeeper may, within his own half of the field of play, use his hands, but shall not carry the ball'. So a goalkeeper could handle the ball anywhere in his own half, not just within the penalty area as today.

As a result of this Roose was able to completely legally undertake a manoeuvre that must have seemed strange even at the time, and would today be completely outrageous. He would first bounce the ball to the halfway line, rather like a basketball player, and then would either punt or throw the ball upfield to be intercepted by his teammates.

As unusual as Roose's methods might have been, they worked to such an extent that, following an extremely successful time at Aberystwyth, there were calls for Roose to represent Wales at the Home International Championship in 1900. In the end, Fred Griffiths, who played for Blackpool, was selected instead. However, following a disastrous match against Scotland in which Griffiths played rather poorly, contributing to a 5-2 loss for Wales, it was decided that Roose should be given the chance to play for his country after all. It was announced that he would be in goal when Wales played Ireland in Llandudno for the next match in the competition.

This time things went better for Wales and they won the match 2-0. In typical fashion, Roose made a memorable international debut; at one point in the match Ireland's Harry O'Reilly launched an attack down the right wing. Roose hurried to intercept him, knocking into him so hard that he was rendered unconscious. While today that would be considered appalling, the referee neither awarded a free kick nor ruled that Roose had committed a foul. Although Wales did not go on to win the Home International Championship, there was still plenty for Roose to be cheerful about, as the following month Aberystwyth Town won the Welsh Cup. Nevertheless, Roose left the club at the end of the season in order to work as an assistant at King's College Hospital, London – he wanted to study medicine but since all the degree places had already been taken that year, this was the next best thing.

Roose continued playing amateur football during this period, joining London Welsh (a team for native

Welsh players living in the capital, not to be confused with the modern rugby union team). The standard of play was not as high as Roose was used to, but playing on the team was no bad thing for his profile; spectators and sports journalists began to flock to see Roose and his inimitable style of play. It wasn't long before clubs began to approach him in the hopes of persuading him to sign a contract and go professional. Roose resisted all such offers as a professional career would interfere with his plan to study medicine.

In fact it was an offer of a different sort that eventually proved convenient for Roose. Stoke didn't have the funds to compete with the richest clubs when it came to acquiring players. They were keen to find skilled amateurs who would play for expenses. Leigh agreed to join the team on the condition that he could continue living in London and working at the hospital. They agreed, and offered him a vast expense account to cover first-class travel, stays in luxurious hotels and other such incentives.

Stoke were a First Division club but they were not one of the strongest – in fact they were in danger of relegation. The 1901–02 season did not get off to a good start, either for Roose or Stoke. Roose was forced to miss several games: due to food poisoning; due to accusations (later rebuffed) that he had played in a qualifying round for London Welsh and so could not do the same that season for Stoke; and also due to his commitments at King's College Hospital. Stoke lost a depressing seven games in a row.

By the time they faced Bolton Wanderers on 9 April 1902, relegation was looking very likely for the club, if they were unable to turn things around. Bolton dominated the first half of the game, repeatedly breaking through to make attempts on goal. However, they were unable to get anything past Roose and, heartened by this, Stoke pushed back hard in the second half, ending up with a very comfortable 4-0 victory. The following Saturday, they saw off Grimsby Town 2-0: Stoke had been saved from relegation, thanks in large part to Roose. He was now a nationally recognised footballer.

It was a turning point in his career. He had been scheduled to begin his course in medicine in October 1902, but it was hard for him to turn his back on burgeoning success and the adulation of the crowds. When Stoke's manager, Horace Austerberry, asked him to play for another season he readily agreed, deferring his course for another year and continuing his work as an assistant at the hospital.

From then on Roose experienced a meteoric career

rise. He stuck with Stoke until 1904, making eighty-one appearances for the club, but was then poached by Everton for a single season, after which he returned to Stoke for another two. Following this he undertook a two-season run at Sunderland from 1908–10, and then went on to spend brief stints at Huddersfield Town, Aston Villa and Woolwich Arsenal. He displayed some truly remarkable goalkeeping and set some enviable records; during his time playing for Everton, for example, he did not concede a single goal in eight of his twenty-four appearances.

He continued to play for the Welsh national side throughout his career and seems to have been as instrumental in improving the fortunes of his country's team as he was the fortunes of the domestic clubs he joined. In 1902 he kept a clean sheet in the Home International Championship match between England and Wales, which subsequently ended in a 0-0 draw, becoming the first Welsh goalkeeper to achieve this feat since 1881.

He eventually went on to captain Wales in 1906. As he said himself: 'To play for one's country is an honour, no matter how many times one is selected to appear. To captain one's country is, however, the honour of honours, generating the kind of pride within a man that is difficult to define in words.' The following year, the Welsh team managed to beat Ireland 3-2 and then Scotland 1-0. A 1-1 draw with England in their final match won the Home International Championship for Wales – the first time this had ever happened.

For all his successes, Roose's career was not without its controversies, chief among these being the fact that he retained his amateur status for the span of his career, being paid only in 'expenses'. The fact that the various moves he made between clubs seem to have coincided with those clubs offering more generous expense accounts makes it plain that Roose was a professional footballer in all but name. Given the simmering tensions in the game over the issue of professionalism, as mentioned earlier in this book, it is easy to understand how some people took exception to Roose reaping the benefits of what amounted to a salary while retaining his amateur status.

The FA was under no illusions about the nature of Roose's arrangements with the clubs he played for. In 1908 they decided to launch a formal investigation into the expenses he was being paid. Roose himself produced a list of some of his supposed expenses that quite clearly sent the message 'I don't give a damn'. It included the items:

Pistol to ward off opposition, 4d

Coat and gloves to keep warm when not occupied, 3d

Using the toilet (twice), 2d

It's pretty obvious that Roose was, as it were, 'taking the piss', but when Sunderland, for whom Roose was then playing, were somehow able to produce receipts proving that they only paid for his travel expenses, the FA was left with little option but to back down. Still, the issue continued to raise its head from time to time throughout the rest of Roose's career. For him of course, it was the best of both worlds, since it meant he was able to continue his work and studies at King's College Hospital, where he had started to specialise in bacteriology.

Unsurprisingly his career continued to be characterised by exceptional achievement and a good deal of drama. He stuck to his unusual approach to goalkeeping, and seemed to think that other goalkeepers were a bit feeble for not taking advantage of the freedom of movement in their own half that the rules of the game afforded them. Roose himself stated that:

A goalkeeper should take in the position at once at a glance and, if deemed necessary, come out of his goal immediately. He must be regardless of personal consequences and, if necessary, go head first into a pack into which many men would hesitate to insert a foot, and take the consequent gruelling like a Spartan. I am convinced that the reason why goalkeepers don't come out of their goal more often is their regard for personal consequences. If a forward has to be met and charged down, do not hesitate to charge with all your might.

And it's clear that Roose fully practised what he preached. In November 1905 a reporter in the *Bristol Times* wrote the following about him:

Few men exhibit their personality so vividly in their play as L. R. Roose. You cannot spend five minutes in his company without being impressed by his vivacity, his boldness, his knowledge of men and things – a clever man, undoubtedly, but entirely unrestrained in word or action. He rarely stands listlessly by the goalpost even when the ball is at the other end of the enclosure, but is ever following the play closely. Directly his charge is threatened, he is on the move. He thinks nothing of dashing out 10 or 15 yards, even when his backs have as good a chance of clearing as he makes for himself. He will also rush along the touchline, field the ball and get in a kick too, to keep the game going briskly. Equally daring and unorthodox are his methods of dealing with strong shots. He is not a model custodian by all means. He would not be L. R. Roose if he was.

And Leigh Roose's idiosyncrasies extended beyond the way he physically played the game – he was just as keen to keep the opposing side psychologically off balance. If he was able to do so while indulging in a bit of showboating for the crowds, so much the better. He was a natural entertainer and crowd-pleaser, and was known for sitting on top of his crossbar at half-time, exchanging jokes with the crowd. On one occasion, facing a penalty kick in a match against Manchester City, Roose taunted the penalty taker with exaggerated displays of fear, knocking his knees together and miming being unsteady on his feet. This put his opponent off so badly that he ended up kicking the ball straight at Roose, who saved it easily. Unfortunately the Manchester City supporters did not find this as amusing as Roose himself clearly did, and when he turned, arms upheld in triumph, they pelted him with anything they could get their hands on.

An even more devious psychological game that Roose played was later related by Billy Meredith, a fellow Welsh footballing legend of the time:

> In those days, Wales was never really sure of a first team and there used to be a sigh of relief when the party trickled up in twos or threes. Reserves were usually standing by, but a reserve goalkeeper was not thought of when Dick Roose was holding down the position.
>
> You can imagine the consternation, then, when he turned up at Liverpool for the boat to Belfast with his hand heavily bandaged. He told everybody not to worry, that he'd only broken a couple of bones but would be able to play. Those of us who knew him well were naturally suspicious and when we settled in our hotel at Belfast, Charlie Morris and I peeped through the keyhole of his room and saw him unwind the bandage and exercise his fingers.
>
> Next morning he appeared with his bandage back on and the telegraph wires hummed with the news that the Welsh goalkeeper was going to play with two broken fingers. The photographers crowded round the Welsh goal at the start of the match, but

once the play was in progress Dick calmly unwound
the bandage and went on to play his usual blinder.

While such stunts doubtless irritated plenty of
Roose's opponents and their supporters, they were also
one of the reasons he had such a wildly devoted following. And his life off the pitch was just as outrageous.
That Roose was a tremendous flirt with a great love
of women was common knowledge, and his romantic
life began to interest the public almost as much as his
sporting life. Around the end of 1909 he was linked to
the music hall star Marie Lloyd. The two had been seen
around London together and, since rumour already
had it that Lloyd's second marriage was in trouble, it
was pretty obvious what was going on.

It was all over by summer 1910, but of course it
attracted considerable attention – one of the greatest
footballing stars of the day in a passionate affair with
one of the most famous singers. The comparison with
certain celebrities today is obvious. The relationship
apparently ended when Lloyd met and fell in love with
the jockey Bernard Dillon, whom she would eventually marry. It was not a happy pairing – both Dillon
and Lloyd had drinking problems – and they separated
six years later. Lloyd became a full-blown alcoholic and

died in October 1922, having collapsed on stage.

Whether Roose was broken-hearted at their split we do not know; if he was, he seems to have got over it rapidly. Being linked to Lloyd had done wonders for his public profile outside of football. At Sunderland, where he was playing at the time, the club received floods of fan mail for him from female admirers and the *Daily Mail* named him 'London's most eligible bachelor'. Roose apparently took full advantage of his heart-throb status, travelling to away games a day early in order to spend the extra night in the company of one of his legion of admirers.

But by the end of 1910, things started to go wrong for Roose. On 21 November he was on the Sunderland team facing Newcastle United. With fifteen minutes to go before the end of the match, the score stood at 1-1; both sides were desperate to clinch a win. A shot from Newcastle's Albert Shepherd almost made it past Roose but the maverick goalie managed to keep hold of it, just. Calamity struck, however, when another Newcastle player, John Rutherford, tried to kick the ball out of Roose's hands. Chaos ensued as players from both teams rushed in. When the referee intervened and halted the game, Roose was clutching the ball close with his right arm. His left was broken just above the wrist.

He was, of course, unable to play or continue his work at the hospital while he waited for the injury to heal. Perhaps unsurprisingly for such an energetic, active man, it was a difficult adjustment. He said that: 'All good goalkeepers carry about with them an air of invincibility, so it comes as the strangest sensation that we are mortal after all. It is a helpless predicament and time will determine what happens next.' He must have been wondering what the injury meant for the future of his career, and the press were speculating about the same thing.

It wasn't until January 1911 that the cast was finally removed from Roose's arm, revealing that the muscle had wasted considerably through inactivity. Nevertheless he was impatient to begin playing again and insisted on taking part in a Home International Championship match against Scotland on 6 March. Although the game ended in a 2-2 draw it was obvious to those watching that Roose was far from being at the top of his game, and was obviously in pain when he caught the ball.

The knock-on effect of this was immediate. Upon hearing of his lacklustre performance, Sunderland opted to play it safe by rotating other players in goal. The season ended without Roose having played a single match for Sunderland since his injury. He therefore told them that he was leaving to find a club that would actually use him. He eventually joined Aston Villa, but sadly his performance there remained in marked contrast to the illustrious career he had enjoyed previously. Although the club won a few of its fixtures, in general he was still not playing well, and this was clearly affecting him psychologically; after a 3-2 loss at home to Sheffield Wednesday, Roose slumped head down in the dressing room with tears in his eyes. Following that match one journalist commented, 'It sounds suggestive of sacrilege to say this but Roose on his present form is not the Roose we have been accustomed to see for a number of years, for it seems he has lost his judgement.'

Whether it was the injury itself or the accompanying loss of nerve, Roose was no longer the greatest goalkeeper in the country. He left Aston Villa, having played only ten games for the club, and tried his luck instead with Woolwich Arsenal, generally known simply as 'The Arsenal'. Here his form improved considerably, but in spite of still being a better goalkeeper than many, he was no longer the extraordinary player he had been. When the Football Association of Wales made the shocking announcement that for a Home International Championship game against Scotland in March 1912

Robert Evans, who played for Blackburn Rovers, would be in goal, it could not be a clearer signal that Roose's glory days were over.

Shortly after that, Leigh Richmond Roose finally hung up his boots. In a strangely poignant turn of events, it was in June 1912 that the FA's rules review committee amended Law 8 of the game to: 'The goalkeeper may, within his own penalty area, use his hands, but shall not carry the ball.' Apparently in the preceding years a couple of committee members had been struck by Roose's penchant for bouncing the ball to the halfway line, something which they felt spoilt the game. By limiting the area in which a goalkeeper could handle the ball they hoped to discourage future players from emulating Roose's tactics. Perhaps it was for the best that Roose had been forced to retire – he surely would not have enjoyed the game as much if he had been checked in this way. It is also a testimony to this remarkable maverick player that the rules of the game should have been changed in such a significant way specifically on his account.

For the next couple of years Roose played on a freelance basis for a few clubs in lower leagues, and he also had his medical career and the personal appearances that, as a bona fide sporting legend, he was paid a considerable fee for. But when war broke out Roose, never one to avoid conflict if circumstances required it, joined the Royal Army Medical Corps, where he could put the medical skills he had learned to good use. His minister father was a pacifist and was opposed to his son becoming involved in the war at all. We can probably assume, however, that Roose's decision to go with the intention of saving lives was more palatable to his father than if he had gone to end them.

By October 1914, Roose had left Britain for France. He worked in a hospital close to the town of Rouen, where injured soldiers were brought from the front prior to being transported to one of the main ports for evacuation – if and when they were well enough to travel. However, in March 1915 Roose and several of his colleagues were ordered back to Britain and reassigned. Within a few weeks they were sailing for Egypt, en route to Gallipoli. There they were much more in the thick of things than they had been in France, working in makeshift hospitals extremely close to the fighting.

And the fighting raged almost non-stop. Far from being an easy victory over the Turks, as had been hoped, Gallipoli became a terrible and protracted slaughter for both sides. It is estimated that the Allies suffered as many as 265,000 casualties, and the Turks an even more appalling 300,000. The terrible heat of the summer made the area – strewn with unburied corpses – a perfect breeding ground for disease; more than half the British casualties have been attributed to illnesses such as dysentery and diarrhoea. Roose wrote to his former Sunderland teammate George Holley about the appalling conditions:

> If ever there was a hell on this occasionally volatile planet then this oppressively hot, dusty, diseased place has to be it. If I have seen the fragments of one plucky youth whose body…or what remains of it…has been swollen out of all proportion by the sun, I have seen several hundred. The bombardment is relentless to the extent that you become accustomed to its tune, a permanent rat-a-tat-tat complemented by busting shells.

The fighting dragged on throughout 1915 until Lord Kitchener, the minister for war, came to assess the situation in November. He concurred with Allied commanders that the situation had become untenable and would likely worsen with the coming of winter. He recommended that the campaign be called off and all troops evacuated. The British Cabinet sanctioned this and from December onwards forces began to withdraw from the peninsula. The campaign had been a disaster for the Allies and had diverted much-needed resources from the Western Front.

But what had happened to Leigh Roose? By the beginning of 1916 his family feared the worst. They had not heard from him since before Christmas and, when they enquired, they were told that he had indeed gone missing. After several months they were forced to accept that the former 'Prince of Goalkeepers' was dead, his body lost somewhere amid the chaos and horror of Gallipoli.

In fact, as we will learn later, they were wrong.

5

The Pals Arrive in France

The hoped-for breakthrough in Gallipoli had turned into a catastrophic failure. With that failure came the unwelcome realisation that the war would almost certainly be won or lost on the Western Front, where a bloody stalemate still reigned. The French commander-in-chief Marshal Joseph Joffre and the newly appointed British commander-in-chief Field Marshal Sir Douglas Haig were in agreement: an assault on the largest scale that could be managed should be attempted in spring 1916, as soon as weather conditions became more favourable. Such an assault would require all the troops that could possibly be mustered.

During the course of 1915 the footballers' battalions,

the 17th Middlesex and 16th Royal Scots, had undergone rigorous training. This consisted mainly of building physical fitness, marching, drilling and accustoming recruits to a life of unquestioning obedience. The men were trained in the use of their rifles and other ordnance and were also taught basic wiring and first aid. Considering their existing physical fitness, familiarity with a training regimen and experience of working as a cohesive team, it is probable that professional footballers had some advantage over recruits from other backgrounds. That said, it seemed that in general the men were by no means as disciplined as would have been desirable. Lieutenant Cosmo Clark of the 17th Middlesex wrote that:

My platoon of sixty men are a mixed mob who haven't (through bad teaching) realized what is expected of them as soldiers. In fact, the whole battalion are the same – the majority of the junior officers let unforgivable little crimes slip by without saying anything…During a lecture by a sergeant major on musketry I spotted a man who was actually fitting a live cartridge into the chamber of his rifle! Men were all about him and his rifle was pointing into the midst of them!

And to begin with, the 16th Royal Scots seemed to have had similar difficulties in taking army life very seriously, as was reported in the *Evening News* in February 1915:

> During the first week or two the acting sergeants had a trying time getting the lazy ones to leave the comfort of their blankets. The command of 'show a leg' was looked on as a piece of humour and the funny men would push the blankets to one side to fulfil the command literally.

The punishing training schedule soon knocked some discipline into the men, but while it certainly turned them into better soldiers, it also had a somewhat detrimental effect on the quality of the football they were playing. With the greater part of the Heart of Midlothian team now among the ranks of the 16th Royal Scots, the club was now at a serious disadvantage; its players were frequently ill, indisposed or exhausted as a result of the rigours of army life. On one occasion they had to play having only returned from night manoeuvres just in time to catch the train to the match. It is unsurprising, therefore, that they failed to hold on to their league title that year, conceding it to Celtic.

Meanwhile the 17th Middlesex had formed their own team, which played matches against other battalion teams (of course, given the number of professionals in its ranks, the 17th Middlesex had a distinct advantage in such fixtures), or sometimes against local clubs. The latter were often played primarily in order to aid recruiting and to raise awareness of the footballers' battalion. Such games went on throughout the year, with mixed results; the 17th beat Reading on 4 September and Cardiff City on 4 October, both matches ending 1-0, but lost 3-2 to Luton Town on 11 October and drew with Birmingham the week after.

Unfortunately both battalions took losses of life in 1915 without ever having seen combat. A young lance corporal in the 17th Middlesex, a former shipping clerk named Edward Frost, died of acute meningitis on 26 April. Later in the year the 16th Royal Scots were deprived of a face that was familiar to all Hearts fans – 26-year-old Tom Gracie, the previous season's highest scorer in Scotland, passed away on 23 October in Glasgow. He had secretly been suffering from leukaemia since March but had continued both his sporting and military training in spite of the illness. He had bravely concealed his condition until it was impossible to do so any longer. With Gracie's death, Hearts lost one of their most valued teammates and the 16th Royal Scots a staunch comrade. Both footballing battalions would have to become accustomed to men disappearing from their ranks, however, as their training was coming to an end and soon they would be setting out for the continent – and for war.

The bulk of the 17th Middlesex left from Folkestone on 17 November 1915 on the *Princess Victoria*. Even the seemingly simple operation of crossing the English Channel was potentially hazardous now; the Channel had been mined, and earlier that same day a hospital ship, the *Anglia*, had been sunk after hitting one. Happily no such calamity befell the 17th Middlesex and they disembarked safely at Boulogne in the early hours of 18 November. It wasn't a very comfortable arrival, as it was raining hard and the men were left waiting in the wet for a couple of hours before they at last received orders to make for the nearby rest camp, Ostrohove. The next day they marched to a little village called Les Ciseaux, a mere sixteen miles from the front lines, where they were given billets in barns and other farm buildings. The boom of the artillery was now clearly audible, but as yet they were not being sent into combat. However, it was now only a matter of time.

Naturally the players kept in touch with the people they had left behind. On 7 December, Brighton & Hove Albion goalkeeper Bob Whiting wrote to Albert Underwood, the club secretary, sounding cheerful:

> There are only five of us [from the Brighton & Hove team] out here doing our bit – myself, Booth, Tyler, Woodhouse, and Dexter, and they are very pleased to hear from you, and told me to tell you they are going on fine. I daresay it has been rotten not having or seeing any football. There is plenty out here, and we are receiving challenges every minute of the day. But we are too good for them all. They are trying to pick a team out of the whole Army out here to play us, so it will be a big match, though I think we are certain winners.
>
> Well, we are having some exciting times in the 'big match' out here. It is great sport to see our airmen scoring against the 'Allemanges' [German troops] – hoping you will excuse the bit of French. Going great guns in the French language out here, quite a genius at it. I hope this will find you and all old friends at Brighton in the best of health as it leaves me at present. Am looking forward to be playing next season with the old club.

Over the next two weeks the battalion moved a few times, spending time in the town of Isbergues, the location of a gigantic French munitions factory, the town of Béthune, and finally Annequin, which was only a couple of miles from the front. From there, on the cold wet evening of 10 December, A and B companies of the battalion were sent down into the trenches between Loos and La Bassée to be given their first experience of life on the front. The unpleasant conditions they found themselves in were typical of winter in the trenches – it poured with rain and at times the men found themselves submerged up to their waists in water and mud. Twenty-four hours later, C and D companies of the battalion relieved them.

Tragically C and D's first stint in the trenches was more eventful, and the battalion suffered its first fatality in the field when Private James McDonald was hit by a burst of machine-gun fire while on sentry duty; he had spent only seven hours in the trenches. The fact that a man could be picked off like this when not even involved in an assault (neither side was engaged in major action at this time due to the weather) was a harsh lesson for the 17th in the realities of existence at the front.

Over the coming days the men would all have to

adjust to constant danger and discomfort as unavoidable facts of life, along with the cold and the tormenting lice that soon infested them all. The battalion settled into their routine as best they could, getting up each day before dawn to stand in readiness in case of an attack, and spending the day doing all manner of tasks, from repairing damaged fortifications and digging latrines to maintaining their equipment and tending to the wounded.

Bob Whiting's Brighton & Hove teammate Jack Woodhouse had been writing to Albert Underwood too, putting a brave face on things:

> We have been in the firing line just over a week. It was an exciting experience the first day or so to hear our big guns firing behind us and the whistling and bursting of the German shells overhead, but after the first few days it seemed a matter of course. We have had some miserable and wet weather since we have been here, and the trenches are knee deep in mud, but all the boys seem happy enough.

Meanwhile the cheerfulness was starting to ebb from Whiting's letters:

> We are having a rest after our first dose of the trenches and I can tell you we have earned it ... I can honestly tell you it is all work and very little play. You feel a bit fatigued in the trenches after you have been there for 24 hours building up parapets, which the fellows across the way knock down with their whizzbangs.

Bob Whiting had been born in Canning Town in East London on 6 January 1883. His football career began when, as a young man, he found work with the Thames Ironworks and Shipbuilding Company. There he joined the company football team, which had recently been renamed – it was now called West Ham United. Standing six foot tall and weighing around twelve stone gave Bob a natural advantage when it came to playing in goal. Despite this he only ever made West Ham's reserve team. It was likely frustration at this that caused him to move to Kent-based Tunbridge Wells Rangers after a couple of years. While playing for Tunbridge on 13 January 1906 he was spotted by scouts from Chelsea; shortly afterwards he signed as their reserve goalkeeper. Fortunately for Whiting, the Chelsea goalkeeper, Micky Byrne, was injured in the first match of the 1906–07 season and Whiting was given the chance he needed to establish himself as the starting goalie. Between 1906 and 1908 he continued to play for Chelsea, earning himself the nickname 'Pom Pom', after the naval gun of the same name, due to the range and power of his kicks.

He subsequently joined Brighton & Hove Albion in the summer of 1908, where he played as the first team's goalkeeper. He made a total of 320 appearances for the club, a record that would not be surpassed for over 50 years. During the 1909–10 season he conceded just 28 goals in 42 matches. That season ended with Albion winning the Southern League Championship. He joined the 17th Middlesex at the first recruitment meeting at Fulham Town Hall on 15 December 1915.

Whiting had left behind a young family in England: his wife Nellie, whom he had married in 1907, and two young sons. But he was not to be separated from them for very long, as he was among the first of the battalion to succumb to one of the many maladies that were a risk in the trenches: in May, a few months after his arrival, Whiting contracted scabies. He was invalided home and sent to the Eastern Military Hospital in Brighton in order to recover. There events took an unexpected and, doubtless in the eyes of some, undistinguished turn.

Nellie was able to come and stay in Brighton and to see Bob while he was recovering. During the time they spent together she fell pregnant, but once Bob was recovered he was inevitably to be sent back to the front. It seems that the idea of leaving Nellie to have their third child alone was more than he could stand; he went absent without leave from the hospital. This was a serious military crime for which he could face death if caught. Such an action would inevitably attract calls of cowardice, though it seems a harsh condemnation of a man who seems to have acted primarily out of love of his family.

Whiting's whereabouts might have remained unknown indefinitely. However, like his fellow goalkeeper Leigh Roose, this was not the end of Whiting's war story – we will hear more of it in due course.

The experience of the 16th Royal Scots, McCrae's battalion, was similar to that of the 17th Middlesex. They had concluded their training and left for the continent somewhat later, boarding the paddle steamer *Empress Queen* at Southampton on 8 January 1916, bound for Le Havre. Interestingly, a couple of weeks previously it had been far from certain that the battalion would be joining the struggle on the Western Front. On

18 December they had been issued with sun helmets and tropical uniforms, and it was rumoured that their first port of call would be Egypt. A week later, however, the uniforms were recalled and France became the battalion's definite destination.

They disembarked at Le Havre around dawn and marched to a rest camp. The next day they caught a train to Saint-Omer, though 'caught a train' perhaps implies a greater level of comfort than the battalion was afforded: the officers were at least able to squeeze into a small second-class carriage, but the rest of the men were forced to endure transport in strawless cattle trucks. Upon arrival in Saint-Omer, and without having eaten, they then had to march fifteen miles to their billets in a village called Wallon-Cappel. There followed several days of route marches, training and general acclimatisation – this particular part of the line, in the Armentières section of French Flanders, was relatively quiet and therefore a suitable place for the men to be given their first taste of the war. However, the comparative safety could not last for ever, and after some time moving billets from village to village the battalion was ordered to Fort Rompu, just west of the front line. On 27 January they entered the line themselves.

The fortifications behind which they huddled were

necessarily somewhat different to the norm here; the water table in the area was too high to allow for the digging of trenches, which would immediately become canals, and so breastworks – earthen walls about five feet high – had been piled up instead. The battalion would need whatever protection they could find because that night, the Germans let rip with a tremendous bombardment, the worst ever experienced on that part of the line. The 16th Royal Scots were given a literal baptism of fire, shells raining down throughout the night. There was a brief let-up in the early hours of the morning but the guns started up again just after breakfast and continued all day. It must have been a hellish 24 hours, and unsurprisingly the battalion did not escape unscathed – Robert Russell, a mechanic from Dunfermline who was just nineteen years old, was killed by a high-explosive shell that landed in the doorway of his shelter.

Thankfully the following days did not see a repeat of this dreadful experience, but the men of the 16th Royal Scots could no longer be under any illusions about what the coming months had in store for them, or how easily any one of them might lose his life.

So by February both the main footballing pals battalions had experienced the shock of combat, and both had lost their first men in the line of duty. As winter came to an end, the Allied command were still finalising plans for their scheduled large-scale offensive in the spring. During discussions at Chantilly in December 1915 it had been agreed that the area around the River Somme would be the location for the push on the Western Front. The French would undertake the main offensive, supported on their northern flank by the British. At the same time, the other Allied powers, Italy and Russia, would begin offensives on their own fronts. Unfortunately the Germans and their allies had plans of their own. On 21 February they began a tremendous artillery attack on Verdun and the surrounding area, which contained a large number of French forts that historically had protected France's eastern border. This opening bombardment lasted a solid ten hours, during which 808 guns fired an astonishing one million shells.

The offensive had been conceived by the German Chief of the General Staff, Erich von Falkenhayn. He was convinced that, because of their historical significance, the French would be anxious to protect the forts at any cost rather than face the national humiliation of conceding them. They would therefore single-mindedly commit all the men they could muster to the area's defence, and these men could then be slaughtered by the massed fire of the German artillery, which was considerably better supplied with ammunition than that of the Allies.

The initial attack fell like a hammer blow on the French at Verdun, who were largely unprepared. One French soldier wrote of the horror of being on the receiving end of this bombardment: 'Men were squashed. Cut in two or divided from top to bottom. Blown into showers; bellies turned inside out; skulls forced into the chest as if by a blow from a club.' In the face of a devastating wall of firepower there was little that the French could do at first, and the Germans made significant gains that included the capture of the great fort at Douaumont, which had been considered impregnable. However, although the French were forced back they did not break, and their hastily arranged countermeasures, overseen by General Petain, managed to check the German advance. Like so many of the battles in the First World War, Verdun now became a grinding war of attrition.

The powerful German artillery had cut off all methods of supply and communication to Verdun bar one extremely narrow road, which would become known as the Voie Sacrée, the 'Sacred Way', so vital was it to the French army's defensive efforts. With only this one lifeline to sustain them, the situation was severe. Conditions for French troops on the ground were appalling, with one soldier saying: 'You eat beside the dead, you drink beside the dead, you relieve yourself beside the dead and you sleep beside the dead.' And another: 'Hell cannot be so terrible as this. Humanity is mad; it must be mad to do what it is doing.' But in spite of the monstrous things they had to endure, through a combination of clever tactics and the sheer stubborn courage of men fighting to defend their homeland, the French continued to hold off the German offensive. The terrible battle would last for much of 1916.

Given that the fighting at Verdun took place between the French and German armies, one might wonder why it is relevant in a book about British soldiers – and in particular about British footballer-soldiers. The answer is that it took a titanic effort for the French to hold Verdun, with many French divisions which had been intended to take part in the planned Allied assault on the Somme being diverted there. As a result the British offensive, rather than supporting the French, became the principal effort, and a tremendous number of British troops were therefore soon to take the lead in one of the biggest offensives the British army had ever attempted. The players in the 17th Middlesex and the

16th Royal Scots, as well as numerous other footballers in other regiments, were going to be in the thick of it. There were still several months of preparation before the offensive could begin, but in the meantime the men had plenty to occupy themselves.

For the 17th Middlesex this included the conclusion of the army's divisional football tournament. This competition had started in January and in their first match the battalion's team – composed of players from a range of clubs including Reading, Chelsea, Huddersfield Town, Clapton Orient, Luton Town and Southend United – had predictably thrashed the team fielded against them by the 13th Essex, winning 9-0. This rather set the tone for the rest of the competition, and over the coming months the 17th Middlesex defeated the 2nd South Staffords and 1st King's Royal Rifle Corps convincingly before smashing the 34th Brigade Royal Field Artillery 11-0 in the final on 11 April. Across the tournament the team had scored 44 goals without reply. Of course they had an unfair advantage, and no one can have thought for a moment that any other team stood a chance, but for the men of the other divisions it must have been a tremendous thrill to play against a collection of sporting icons, no matter how soundly they were beaten.

Some weeks after winning this honour the 17th Middlesex distinguished themselves again, but this time in combat. The part of the Western Front that included Vimy Ridge, an escarpment north-east of Arras, had been held by the Germans since October 1914 and, aside from a couple of French attempts to take it back in May and September 1915, had remained a relatively quiet part of the line. This comparative calm had been capitalised upon by the Germans, who had begun mining operations, constructing a network of tunnels under the battlefield which could be used to detonate explosives beneath the French positions.

However, when British forces relieved the French in February 1916 the Royal Engineers immediately began their own counter-mining operations, deliberately collapsing any German tunnels they were able to detect. It didn't take long for the Germans to lose patience and on 21 May, having unleashed an intense volley of artillery and trench mortars over the preceding days, they launched a concentrated attack on the British positions. The German bombardment had been so effective that whole sections of the British line had been destroyed and the men still in position were unable to offer effective resistance – many were captured. The 2nd Division of the Third Army of the BEF were in reserve around ten miles away and were urgently ordered to Vimy to offer support. The 17th Middlesex were part of that division.

The fighting continued over the next few days as the British hastily counter-attacked, failing to dislodge the Germans from the ground they had gained and sustaining heavy casualties in the process. The 17th Middlesex were not involved in that action, but soon found themselves in the thick of things when they relieved the 13th Essex on 30 May. The part of the line they took over was at the northern end of Vimy Ridge and had not been subjected to the withering hail of German artillery on 21 May. As a result the British tunnels in this region were intact and could still be used for further mining operations. The 176th Tunnelling Company began to prepare three mines for detonation.

The plan was that these would be exploded on 1 June, following an artillery bombardment. The combination of the three would, it was assumed, completely wipe out the German front lines, ensuring that an infantry attack by the 1st King's (Liverpool) Regiment, supported by the 17th Middlesex, would meet relatively little resistance. Everything proceeded according to schedule, with the British artillery bombardment beginning just after 4 p.m. and, predictably, being met with a reply from the German guns. This continued throughout the afternoon and early evening until, at 8.30 p.m., the three mines were detonated. Second Lieutenant Cosmo Clark of the 17th Middlesex described the scene:

> At eight thirty our mines went up and I had a splendid view of them. They don't make much noise but they make the ground rock backwards and forwards for a good half minute. All you can see of the explosion is an immense tongue of flame about twice the size of our house. Great chunks of earth flew into the air like so much paper, as did some Bosche spread-eagled against the sky. Then the Bosche started with his artillery. The shells simply came over and burst in thousands – great flashes everywhere which burned one's skin and yet the bits of metal that flew around missed one.

When the retaliatory fire died down, the British infantry raiding parties set out. It soon became apparent that while the German artillery had done considerable damage to the British lines, the same could not be said for the effect of the British artillery and the mines: German defences were still largely intact and the advancing British troops were met with heavy machine-gun fire. It was obvious that it would not be possible to storm the German front lines and so the securing of the lips of the newly created mine craters, which had originally been undertaken only by covering parties, now became the main objective.

A terrible night of fighting followed, with the Germans determinedly trying to drive the men of the 17th from the edge of the crater with bombs, and the 17th holding them off with Lewis guns while trying to construct a new line of defence. In fact the Germans still continued to press forward and it was only a courageous counter-attack of bombers led by Sergeant Charles Cook that managed to keep them at bay. We can only imagine what it must have been like to be out there that night, dodging the bullets as explosions rent the darkness. It was tremendously hazardous work and unsurprisingly the footballers' battalion began to suffer significant casualties. Private Angus Seed, a Reading player, distinguished himself by dragging a number of wounded men back to the British dugouts, among them Private Thomas Ratcliff, an assistant trainer for Arsenal. He and Charles Cook were among seven members of the battalion to be decorated subsequently with the Military Medal for their actions that night. Three officers who had commanded the attack – Captain William Salter,

Captain Thomas Rollason and Second Lieutenant John Engleburtt – were all awarded the Military Cross.

But these honours came at a price. Although the number of casualties was not as high as it might have been, three officers and five other ranks were killed; one officer and thirty-eight other ranks were wounded. Among those killed was Herbert Derisley, honorary steward of Crystal Palace, while among the wounded were Corporal Billy Baker, who played for Plymouth Argyle, and Private Thomas Codd, who played for Leicester Fosse. For the next couple of days the battalion spent time consolidating the positions they had succeeded in gaining, during which time one of the craters from the exploded mines was christened 'Football Crater'. They were relieved on 3 June 1916 by the 13th Essex.

The footballers' battalion of the Middlesex had now carried out their first major operation, and they had every reason to be proud of the way they had conducted themselves. Major General William Walker, who commanded the 2nd Division to which the battalion belonged, wrote in his report: 'This is the first occasion on which the 17th Middlesex have been engaged in serious fighting, but I consider that they carried out the operation with steadiness and gallantry under very trying circumstances.'

6

The First Day of the Somme

By spring 1916, arrangements for the major offensive on the Somme were nearing completion. Nevertheless, when Field Marshal Haig, commander-in-chief of the British army, met his French opposite number, Marshal Joffre, in the last week of May he had tried to convince the French commander to delay the attack until August. Joffre would not countenance this; the Somme offensive was desperately needed to force the Germans to lessen their persistent assault on Verdun.

In June, therefore, final deployment orders for troops began to be issued – by the end of the month there were twenty-six British and fourteen French divisions in the area, in contrast to only six German divisions. Final preparations were also made for a colossal preliminary bombardment. For the first years of the war the British army had been forced to work under fairly severe ammunition constraints in comparison to the Germans. However, the last year or so had seen the munitions industry at home transformed, with women working in their thousands in the factories for the first time. As a result there was now sufficient ammunition to unleash a storm of artillery along the entire fourteen-mile stretch of front from Serre to Maricourt, which had been chosen for the coming assault.

Accordingly, on 24 June 1916 approximately 1,000 field guns began to shell the German positions with the aim of obliterating their lines to allow an infantry assault to break through, opening the way for cavalry divisions to spill out into open country. The bombardment lasted all day and continued without let-up for days on end. The thunder of the massed guns was earth-shakingly loud, so much so that it could apparently even be heard across the Channel in England. Over the course of a week an estimated 1.6 million shells were fired.

A massive infantry attack was planned for 1 July. The night before, General Haig wrote in his diary:

With God's help I feel hopeful. The men are in splendid spirits. Several have said that they have never before been so instructed and informed of the nature of the operation before them. The wire has never been so well cut, nor the Artillery preparation so thorough.

General Henry Rawlinson also took the time to record the following in his diary:

What the actual result will be, none can say, but I feel confident of success myself, though only after heavy fighting. That the Boche will break and that a debacle will supervene I do not believe, but, should this be the case, I am quite ready to take full advantage of it... The issues are in the hands of the Bon Dieu.

The commanders might have felt that things were set up as well as they could be. Unfortunately, however, a severe error that would cost a great many British lives was about to be made. On the night of 30 June, a German listening post near La Boisselle managed to pick up part of a telegraph message from General Rawlinson to all the men of the Fourth Army. It went as follows:

In wishing all ranks good luck, the Army commander desires to impress on all infantry units the
supreme importance of helping one another and
holding on tight to every yard of ground gained. The
accurate and sustained fire of the artillery should
greatly assist the task of the infantry.

Given that it contained sensitive information, this
message should have been sent out by hand but, concerned that it might not reach all units in time, a staff
officer had used a field telephone instead. The enemy
was now expecting the attack the following day.

That day, which would see bloodshed on an almost
unprecedented scale, dawned fresh and bright, the
sky a brilliant shimmering blue. It might have been a
peaceful summer morning but for the boom of artillery, which had replaced the gentle trills of birdsong; at
6.30 a.m., according to plan, the shelling of the German
forward positions intensified. All along the British line,
men steeled themselves for what they were about to do;
it is hard to imagine that many had slept much during
the night.

That said, there was a certain amount of assur-
ance among the British troops – they had seen and
heard the fearsome bombardment of the enemy

lines and therefore had reason to hope that the bulk of the German defences had indeed been destroyed. With particular confidence one captain in the 8th East Surreys, Billy Nevill, had brought a couple of footballs for his men, apparently thinking that the German resistance might be so minimal as to allow them to pass the balls between each other during the advance. On one he had written 'The Great European Cup-Tie Final, East Surreys v Bavarians, Kick Off at Zero' while on the other he had written simply 'No Referee'.

The infantry attack began at 7.30 a.m., accompanied by the detonation of seventeen mines, which had been prepared along the front of the assault. One of the largest of these mines – planted at the Hawthorn Ridge Redoubt, a German fortification west of Beaumont-Hamel – contained over 30,000 pounds of explosives. When it detonated, flinging earth 4,000 feet into the air, it was perhaps the largest man-made explosion the world had ever seen. The celebrated war photographer Geoffrey Malins recorded the event, and later described the experience of watching it:

> The ground where I stood gave a mighty convulsion.
> It rocked and swayed. I gripped hold of my tripod to
> steady myself. Then, for all the world like a gigantic

sponge, the earth rose high in the air to the height of hundreds of feet. Higher and higher it rose, and with a horrible grinding roar the earth settled back upon itself, leaving in its place a mountain of smoke.

As the din and the shuddering of the ground subsided, officers in the British trenches placed their whistles in their mouths and blew, signalling the advance. Treating this as something like the referee's whistle for kick-off, Captain Billy Nevill led his men out of the trenches and punted one of the balls towards the German lines. It was a daring start to the attack, but sadly did not presage an easy victory.

Some days later, on 12 July, the *Daily Telegraph* ran the following write-up of what happened:

As the company formed on emerging from the trench, the platoon commanders kicked off, and the match against Death commenced. The gallant captain himself fell early in the charge, and men began to drop rapidly under the hail of machine-gun bullets. But still the footballs were booted onwards, with hoarse cries of encouragement or defiance, until they disappeared in the dense smother behind which the Germans were shooting. Then, when the bombs and bayonets had done their work, and the enemy had cleared out, the Surrey men looked for their footballs, and recovered them in the captured traverses. These will be sent to the Regimental Depot at Kingston as trophies worth preserving.

Even as Billy Nevill and other members of the battalion fell, the rest bravely pressed on. However, it became clear that the German trenches had not been as thoroughly devastated as was hoped. Certainly the massive bombardment had caused a great deal of destruction, but many of the German dugouts were deep under the ground – some as far as 30 feet down – making them extremely hard to destroy. Periods of bad weather during the bombardment had also made it hard to assess exactly what damage was being caused and where to redirect the guns. There was significant destruction, but it was not enough to prevent the German troops from mounting a serious defence. Men began to fall in droves.

Thirty-two-year-old Lieutenant Evelyn Henry Lintott was with the 15th Battalion West Yorkshire Regiment, also known as the Leeds Pals. A talented defender, he had been playing for Leeds at the outbreak of war but duly enlisted on 14 September 1914.

Lintott had had a long and distinguished football career, which began with playing part-time for Woking; he captained the team in the 1905–06 season. He then joined Plymouth Argyle in the Southern League, and though he only played twice for the club in 1906 he also gained his first England amateur cap that year, playing left-half in a match against France that England won with a convincing 15-0 scoreline. In 1907 he moved to Queen's Park Rangers, Plymouth's main league rivals, and in 1908 he was selected for the full England side rather than the amateur-only. In doing so he became the first player from QPR to ever play for England; it would also be more than 60 years before another player from the club would make the squad.

On 15 February 1908 England faced Ireland in Belfast and managed to defeat them 3-1. Lintott played well – *The Times* dubbed it 'a most promising first appearance in international football' – and so he kept his place on the team for England's next match on 16 March against Wales, in which they triumphed 7-1. Playing left-back, Lintott had been tasked with marking the legendary Billy Meredith, a Welshman who was signed to Manchester United at the time. Lintott performed his duty so efficiently that, as FA secretary Frederick Wall later wrote, 'At last the patience of Meredith gave out and he turned on Lintott with these words: "Go away, you confounded schoolboy. Go away! Do you hear? You have got seven cursed goals, how many more do you want?"'

Lintott's talents did not go unnoticed by other clubs and towards the end of 1908 he was approached by Bradford City, who had just won promotion to the First Division. He readily agreed to play for them. Until this point in his career Lintott had remained an amateur. However, at the instigation of the management at QPR, who were not doing well financially, he turned professional at this point so that the club would be able to demand a fee for him from Bradford.

Bradford City initially found the adjustment to First Division football far from straightforward and at the end of the season they escaped relegation by the narrowest of margins. However, their form improved considerably in the following seasons, finishing seventh in the First Division the next year and fifth the year after – a year in which they also managed to win the FA Cup. Unfortunately Lintott was not in the squad for the FA Cup final against Newcastle United, having sustained a serious injury during a game at Bolton. This injury would subsequently cause him to lose both confidence and form.

Lintott turned out fifty-three times for Bradford City before accepting an offer from Leeds City, a Second Division club, in June 1912. His debut appearance was in a 4-0 match at Fulham, the *Leeds Mercury* saying afterwards: 'Lintott had always played magnificently. Strong in defence, he also found the opportunity to do nearly all the dangerous shooting that was accomplished on behalf of Leeds.' The paper also praised him for the excellent example he set as the new team captain. He sprang back into great form, apparently fully recovered from his injury. Given that Leeds had been forced to apply for re-election to the league, the fact that in Lintott's first season with them the club finished sixth was quite the result for him.

Unfortunately the 1913–14 season did not go as well for Lintott. Having played almost exclusively as centre-half for the club he was now moved to right wing-back so that another player, Jack Hampson, could take up the position. Although this had been his usual position in his Bradford City days, Lintott was now quite obviously unaccustomed to it and his play suffered considerably. The misfortune of his poor performance was compounded when he suffered an ankle injury in November and ended up only making six appearances during the season. What might have happened in Lintott's career next is impossible to say – the war intervened, and sadly his final season was far from his most illustrious.

Once war broke out it did not take long for Lintott to decide that his place was in the army; on 14 September 1914 he joined the 15th West Yorkshires at Leeds, setting off a couple of weeks later to begin training in the Yorkshire Dales. Lintott obviously took to army life and impressed his superiors, as he was soon promoted to sergeant and eventually, on 20 December, to lieutenant. This made him the first professional footballer to gain a commission.

It was in December 1915 that the 15th West Yorkshires left England behind, their training over. Unlike so many other battalions, their initial destination was not France or Belgium; instead, when they boarded at Liverpool their destination was northern Africa. They were heading to Egypt to defend the Suez Canal from a possible attack from the forces of the Ottoman Empire. The battalion spent three months there before being transported to Marseilles in March 1916, part of the large-scale massing of forces for the attack on the Somme.

So it was that Lintott was there to join the charge on 1 July. He did not survive long, cut down by machine-gun fire as he led an advance on the village of Serre. A description of his death was subsequently printed in the *Yorkshire Post*:

> Lieutenant Lintott's end was particularly gallant. Tragically, he was killed leading his platoon of the 15th West Yorkshire Regiment, The Leeds Pals, over the top. He led his men with great dash and when hit the first time declined to take the count. Instead, he drew his revolver and called for further effort. Again he was hit but struggled on but a third shot finally bowled him over.

On the 8 July, *The Times* ran a brief obituary:

LIEUTENANT EVELYN H. LINTOTT, West Yorkshire Regiment, killed on July 1, was son of Mr Arthur Lintott, of Godalming, and was a famous international Association Football player. As an amateur he was included in the Queen's Park Rangers team, and did so well at half-back that he was chosen to play for England in all three international matches in 1908. Becoming a professional on joining Bradford City next season, he took part in the matches against Ireland and Scotland. In all five engagements he had Warren and Wedlock as his colleagues in the half-back line. A left half of good physique, possessing great skill, Lintott was unfortunate in being hurt several times, or he would no doubt, have played in more representative matches. Entering the Army after the outbreak of the war, he was not long in gaining a commission.

Lintott's body was never recovered. He is commemorated on the Thiepval Memorial to the Missing of the Somme, one of the thousands of British troops who fell in the hail of German bullets that answered the Allied advance. All along the Somme valley that morning, the young men of the nation were cut down in droves.

McCrae's battalion, the 16th Royal Scots, were at the Somme too, and took more than their share of casualties. Having spent the previous months rotating in and out of the trenches close to the nearby town of Albert, they had been at hand for the big push.

The battalion faced a formidable defensive line. La Boisselle, which was one of the Royal Scots' objectives, was a particularly strong position for the Germans, with large deep dugouts connected by underground passages. Pulleys and slides had been installed in the dugouts' shafts, enabling the machine-gunners to leave them near instantaneously in order to engage in combat. La Boisselle itself was situated upon a ridge, with deep valleys flanking both its sides. The British nicknamed these two valleys 'Sausage' (South) and 'Mash'. An attack along them would be extremely dangerous due to the copious numbers of German machine guns that were posted in vantage points; it had been hoped that the artillery would have done enough to clear these out.

As the 16th Royal Scots advanced they experienced little resistance from the trenches immediately in front of them – the bombardment seemed to have done its work here at least – however, as they were closing in, machine-gun fire opened up on their flank and began to scythe through them, felling men like heads of wheat. They grimly persevered in spite of this and managed to gain the enemy trenches.

But if the front line had fallen quickly, the second and third lines were a much more complex affair. Once British soldiers moved on, the Germans were moving through the network of communication trenches to reoccupy positions they had been driven from, creating pockets of resistance and cutting British companies off from one another. Still the attack went on, the British driving German troops from their positions at the cost of monstrous losses to themselves, with whole battalions being all but wiped out.

The players from Heart of Midlothian in the 16th Royal Scots had generally stuck together. Inside forward Henry Wattie and full-back Duncan Currie – who it has previously been noted were among the first Hearts players to enlist – were in the battalion's C company, together with Ernest Ellis, originally a bootmaker by trade, who had played for Norwich and Barnsley before transferring to Hearts. C company fared reasonably well to begin with and so felt able to press on with their advance in spite of the slaughter suffered by both sides.

Like so many others, however, as they moved forward they were suddenly ripped into by unexpected machine-gun fire. Ellis was struck first and went down, followed rapidly by Currie and Wattie. Three of Hearts' greatest players had been felled in less than a minute. The tragedy of Ellis's death was compounded by the fact that, shortly before he left for the front, his wife Isobel had announced that she was pregnant. Ellis would never meet his daughter.

As is the case with so many others, the bodies of these three brave men were never recovered. They too are remembered on the Thiepval Memorial.

All across the battlefield similar stories were playing out as the blood of young men in their prime was spilled on those fields far from home. So similar are the tragic ends to each man's story that it becomes almost repetitious to relate them, but perhaps that in itself serves to remind us of the horrifying scale of the killing that day.

Another footballer who made the ultimate sacrifice was the Irish inside left Bernard 'Barney' Donaghy. Born on 23 December 1882, he started his career at Derry Celtic and went on to play for a variety of prominent clubs – Glentoran, Hibernian, Manchester United and Burnley. He had a very brief international career while playing for Derry Celtic – on 9 August 1902 he made his first and only appearance for Ireland in a match against Scotland at the Balmoral Showgrounds. Ireland unfortunately lost 3-0. Interestingly, this game was only recently declared an official international game by FIFA so at the time no caps were awarded to the players. Donaghy featured twice for the Irish League representative team while registered with Derry Celtic, competing against the Scottish League in a 3-0 loss on 15 February 1902 in Dundee, and against the English League in a 4-0 loss on 14 October 1905 in Manchester.

Looking at his career with the benefit of hindsight, perhaps the most significant portion of it is the short period he spent at Manchester United (which had only changed its name from Newton Heath a few years before) in the 1905–06 season. Donaghy debuted for the club in a Second Division home match against Lincoln City on 4 November 1905, which United won 2-1. Donaghy only turned out twice more for the club that season but it was a highly significant time for United: at the end of the season they achieved promotion to the First Division and began their journey to becoming the astonishingly successful club they are today.

At the outbreak of war Donaghy, who had by now returned to Derry and was married to his long-term sweetheart Sarah, enlisted into the ranks of the 2nd Battalion Royal Inniskilling Fusiliers. Donaghy spent time on the bloody Gallipoli peninsula, where he sustained a head injury from a piece of flying shrapnel. While recovering in Egypt he wrote to Sarah. While she must have been relieved he was alive, his honesty about the situation cannot have been very reassuring: 'The other four soldiers that were beside me were killed. It was an awful sight. I am sure it was the prayers that saved me.'

But if prayers had helped him on that occasion, they would not be enough when Donaghy and his battalion travelled to France to take part in the 1 July attack. The 2nd Inniskilling Fusiliers formed part of the 29th Division, which together with the 4th Division were responsible for mounting attacks on both sides of the village of Beaumont-Hamel. They were cut to pieces by the German defenders; the fatalities to the Royal Inniskilling Fusiliers on that one day amounted to twenty officers and 548 other ranks. Bernard Donaghy was among those brought down. He is yet another whose body was lost to the chaos of the battlefield and whose name is listed on the Thiepval Memorial.

Sadly the same is true of the final player we shall mention, William Sharpley. His football career was brief and relatively unremarkable, all things considered, but his military career and an event that occurred after his death make his story worth recounting.

Sharpley was born in 1892 in Bow, East London, and he was a talented enough left-back to be recruited by Leicester Fosse (now Leicester City), then a Second Division team. In the end, Sharpley only featured once for the first team, playing in a home match on 27 April 1912 against Leeds City, which Leicester won 2-1.

Shortly after this, Sharpley turned his back on the

world of association football. He enlisted in the army well before the war began, joining the 2nd Battalion Essex Regiment as a private. But he continued to pursue his passion for the game while serving, establishing himself in the regimental football team and representing them in at least one match (in February 1914, against Aldershot Command). He was obviously a good all-round sportsman as he also boxed for the regiment in the light heavyweight category.

By the time war broke out in 1914 Sharpley had already been promoted to the rank of sergeant. He and his battalion set off for France almost at once, part of the initial British Expeditionary Force. Over the following months the battalion took part in some of the most famous and deadly engagements of the first months of the war – including the Battle of Le Cateau, the Battle of the Marne, the Battle of Messines and the Battle of Armentières. Within this period, Sharpley was recognised in dispatches for his courageous conduct. When he returned to England for a time, he was made command sergeant major of the 3rd (Reserve) Battalion and awarded the Russian Medal of St George, second class, for bravery in the field. Moreover, he was subsequently presented with the Distinguished Conduct Medal – which was second only to the Victoria Cross

– for, as the *London Gazette* reported in 1916: 'conspicuous gallantry in rescuing and bringing across the open and under fire a wounded N. C. O.'

By 1 July 1916, therefore, Sharpley was regarded as a veteran and a valuable role model for young soldiers, despite being only twenty-four years old. Yet all his experience could not save him as his battalion attacked the area between Serre and Beaumont-Hamel. They entered the fray with twenty-four officers and 606 other ranks. At the end of the day only two officers and 192 other ranks had avoided becoming casualties. Sharpley was not one of that fortunate group and his body was lost somewhere out in the dreadful melee.

The sad story of Sharpley's death has a rather unusual postscript. His sister, Kate, was working as a munitions worker in Woolwich when she received the tragic news and was invited to receive her brother's medals from Queen Mary in a ceremony at Buckingham Palace. She accepted, but it seems that she was overwhelmed with grief and resentment at her brother's death; when the Queen presented her with the medals she flung them back in her face, yelling: 'If you like them so much you can keep them!'

As one can imagine, Kate was quickly removed from the scene. The police beat her quite badly and she was incarcerated for several days. Perhaps surprisingly she was not charged with any criminal offence for the attack, though she did lose her job at the factory. However, the repercussions for her actions certainly didn't transform her into a meek conformist; she became a committed anarchist campaigner and was highly politically engaged until her death in 1978. In acknowledgement of her contributions to the movement throughout her lifetime, in 1979 the Brixton anarchists named their collection of archive material 'the Kate Sharpley Library'.

Although Kate Sharpley had an extreme and public reaction to her brother's death she was hardly alone in having been left devastated by the events of 1 July 1916. The British sustained horrifying losses that day – approximately 58,000 casualties, of which just over 19,000 were deaths. In contrast the German Second Army only sustained in the region of 11,000 casualties. Whole companies of British soldiers were all but completely wiped out. The 16th Royal Scots were a case in point – of the twenty-one officers and 793 other ranks from the battalion who participated in the attack, a staggering twelve officers and 624 other ranks were missing from their companies by the end of the day.

And what had all this spilt blood accomplished?

The gigantic British bombardment at the end of June had failed to cause sufficient damage to the German defences prior to the infantry assault, and indeed must have served to warn them that an attack was imminent – something the intercepted message from General Henry Rawlinson of course confirmed. As we have seen, the result was that the British troops, who were overburdened and expecting relatively little resistance, were mown down in droves by a devastatingly effective response from the German machine guns. Although some gains in territory were made, many of these proved temporary, with subsequent German counter-attacks able to win back lost ground. The French portion of the assault on the southern part of the line fared somewhat better, perhaps partly because German commanders believed that the losses sustained at Verdun would prevent the French from attacking at all. Consequently the French action came as more of a surprise and they were able to achieve most of their objectives.

Ultimately, the decisive breakthrough that Haig and the other commanders had planned and hoped for had not been achieved. In the aftermath of the initial attack, Haig visited the headquarters of the Fourth Army to discuss the renewal of the offensive. He was determined that they would succeed in shattering the German lines. This meant that the stage was set for yet another bloody battle of attrition in a war that had already seen so many. It would require yet more men, including those who had been fortunate enough to have avoided the fighting in the Somme so far, such as the 17th Middlesex. And it would demand yet greater sacrifices.

7

Fields of Slaughter

Donald Simpson Bell was mentioned earlier in this book as one of the first professional players to enlist after the outbreak of hostilities (see page 19). He was playing for Second Division side Bradford when the war began and was only just starting what showed every sign of being a very successful footballing career. However, he did not hesitate to do his duty as he saw it – by 24 October Bell was a lance corporal in the 9th Battalion West Yorkshire Regiment, and was in Surrey to begin his training.

Bell might have continued in the West Yorkshires for the duration of the war had he not happened to bump into an old school friend called Archie White, who was serving as a commissioned officer in the Yorkshire

Regiment, also known as the 'Green Howards'. Surprised that Bell had not secured a commission for himself, White effected an introduction to his commanding officer, Lieutenant Colonel Chapman, who agreed that if Bell made an application to transfer to the Green Howards and become an officer he would support the move. Bell did exactly that, got his commission and by June 1915 had formally joined the 9th Battalion Green Howards. By August the same year, he and the rest of the regiment were on their way to France.

Once on the continent, Bell and his battalion went through the usual process of acclimatisation; at first continuing their training away from the front before being introduced to life in the trenches. Like McCrae's battalion, the Green Howards got their first experience in the lines at Armentières, which was by then a reasonably quiet section of the front for new recruits to cut their teeth on. Once there, they were asked to hold the line while more seasoned troops from the 8th Division attacked further south as part of the Loos offensive, which gave them a first taste of real combat. For the time being, however, they were not ordered into any large-scale offences themselves, and gradually settled into the usual rotation in and out of the trenches that every soldier had to become accustomed to.

Bell took pains to keep abreast of the news from back home, and even wrote on more than one occasion to his local newspaper, the *Harrogate Herald*, who sent a free copy of the paper to every local man at the front and who were happy to publish any correspondence. One such message appeared on 22 December 1915 and describes, among other things, a rather unfortunate side effect of the British artillery's efforts against the German line:

> Lieutenant Donald Bell writes: I had quite a pleasant surprise on Saturday when the mail came in to find a Herald for me, and to see on opening it that I was placed on your list. I have always had the Herald sent to me every week since I enlisted, and I look forward to reading your weekly letter, also those from the 'boys', many of whom I know very well. By means of your paper we are able to keep in touch and know how each is faring. I am very grateful to you for including me in your 'big family', and shall eagerly await the Saturday mail. At the present time I am in the first line trenches, our battalion having relieved the West Yorks, on Friday last.
>
> When we took possession of the trenches we thought we were fortunate to have taken over such

a dry portion of the line, but next morning we had an eye-opener. The Germans hold higher ground than we do, and several streams run from their line to ours. About eight o'clock on the Saturday morning these streams rose rapidly, and in a few moments our trenches were flooded, knee deep, and in some places taking one up to the waist. Until we recognised the danger spots there were frequent mishaps in the way of duckings, one officer breaking the record with three in one day. Since Saturday it has been a case of 'pump, pump, pump', that is, after we had dammed the streams (in more ways than one!), and today the trenches are returning to their former state.

The sudden influx was caused by the bursting of a dam on the German side by means of our artillery. I am afraid the latter did us a bad turn then, but are making up for it this afternoon by shelling the trenches opposite. Sandbags are flying in all directions, and 'Fritz' is having a surfeit of 'iron rations'. This is my first spell in the trenches, but except for the difficulty of keeping dry it has not been an unpleasant experience. I am thankful to know that we shall be out of the trenches for Xmas, and consequently should be able to celebrate the day in a fitting manner. Thanking you once again for your kindness, and wishing you the compliments of the season.

With large offensives winding down in the winter, Bell and his comrades had a relatively uneventful few months – if being constantly under threat from snipers, unexpected bombardments and, indeed, flooded trenches can be described as uneventful. In March 1916 Bell's unit was transferred to the Souchez sector, near the strategically important Vimy Ridge (see page 100), but they were still not involved in any major actions in the first half of the year. At the end of May, Bell was even granted leave and was able to return home for a few precious days. On 5 June he married his sweetheart Rhoda Margaret Bonson, to whom he had proposed before leaving for France for the first time. When he returned to the front, the 9th Green Howards had already moved south to prepare for involvement in the Somme offensive.

The battalion were fortunate enough not to be involved in the first blood-soaked day of the battle; on 1 July they were at rest in the little village of Saint-Saveur some distance away. That night, however, they marched to a wood near Baizieux, closer to the fighting, and on 3 July they moved to a position on a crest overlooking La Boisselle, which had proved to be strategically vital to the German defence effort. The next day some of the battalion attempted a bombing raid on the German positions but were repelled.

It was a day later that Bell carried out the act that would ensure his name would live for ever in history and would lead to him being awarded the highest of all military honours, the Victoria Cross.

One of the features of the local topography was known as 'Horseshoe Trench' – not a trench dug by soldiers but a curved area of high ground between La Boisselle and the nearby Mametz Wood. It was held by the Germans and had significant strategic value. Late in the afternoon on 5 July, Bell and the rest of the 9th Green Howards attacked in the direction of Horseshoe Trench and managed to occupy it in spite of resistance from the enemy. In the process they took 180 prisoners; all seemed to be going well.

Disaster struck when a machine gun opened fire on the left flank of the battalion, who were at that point consolidating their position. Caught out, the Green Howards sustained numerous casualties. Writing to his mother on 7 July, Bell gave his own account of what happened next:

As I told you, the battalion had been in action and did splendidly, capturing a strong German position. I did not go over as I was second in command of the bombers…a machine gun was spotted on the left, which could enfilade the whole of our front. When the battalion went over, I, with my team, crawled up a communication trench and attacked the gun and the trench and I hit the gun first shot from about 20 yards and knocked it over. The G. O. C. [general officer commanding] has been over to congratulate the battalion and he personally thanked me. I must confess it was the biggest fluke alive and I did nothing. I only chucked one bomb but it did the trick. The C. C. [company commander] says I saved the situation for this gun was doing all the damage. I am glad I have been so fortunate for Pa's sake for I know he likes his lads to be top of the tree. He used to be always on about too much play and too little work, but my athletics came in handy this trip. The only thing is I am sore at the elbows and knees with crawling over limestone flints &c. Please don't worry about me, I believe that God is watching over me and it rests with him whether I pull through or not.

Bell is clearly far too modest in his own appraisal of events, perhaps not wanting to be seen as blowing his own trumpet. In fact it is clear from other accounts of what happened that most people did not share his humble opinion of what had occurred. W. H. Breare, a journalist for the *Harrogate Herald* who habitually wrote a letter 'To Our Boys' in the paper, wrote his own version of events in the 19 July 1916 edition of the paper:

Dear Chaps,

It is Friday, and I would have you, even in your minds, with us this day, sharing our joy, our proud elation.

We are hugging ourselves with delight to keep from bursting with satisfaction. I will tell you the story which has given us so much delight. In one of the engagements of the 'push', Second Lieutenant Don Bell's lot were entrusted with the task of taking an important German position. Second Lieutenant Don Bell was in charge of the bombing section. The boys who were to make the rush went on. Soon a German gun was discovered somewhere on their flank enfilading their ranks and doing much damage.

Don Bell took some bombers in the direction of this gun. They crawled on their hands and knees ever so far until within about twenty yards of the offending gun. Bell threw one bomb, and in that first shot blew the gun to smithereens. The party then stormed the German trench and sent fifty Germans below.

Next day the General Officer Commanding came to the regiment and thanked them for the success of that great movement, for it had been entirely successful. He personally thanked Second Lieutenant Don Bell, and the Commanding Officer declared that he had saved the situation. Bell has written a letter home. He tells the outline of the tale, but his narrative was too fettered by modesty. With him was a nice lad of 19, and Bell declares that this lad did all the work – that he did nothing. Moreover, he calls his brilliant shot which destroyed the gun a big fluke. We don't allow anybody to run our boys down, and we could not permit even Bell to depreciate his splendid performance. A fluke indeed! We have only to inquire what a fluke it is to know how far wrong Don is in his estimate. What is a fluke? A fluke is the accomplishment, by an unskilled person, of something for which he had not tried. In other words, an occurrence due to accident rather than skill. Now, too many of us know Don Bell as one of our finest athletes. We know what he has accomplished in the world of sport. We know that he could always throw straight. He could not deny that he tried to hit the gun, or that he did it in the first throw. He is not an unskilled person. Yes, he did try for his objective, and, what is more, succeeded. We are quite ready to give the nice little chap of nineteen every credit for his brave and successful assistance. But Harrogate is jealous of its reputation and its honours, and will not abandon her reflected share of Don Bell's distinction. Undoubtedly Don saved the situation. That is why we are nearly bursting with pride.

But there was a tragic twist in the tale. Breare went on:

It is Monday morning. There is sorrow in our hearts – that which comes with sudden shock, leaving us dazed and quivering from the blow, then, melting with tenderness for those who had the greater right to love him. Don Bell has fallen. A brief telegram tells us so. There is just a gleam of sunshine to lighten our despair. In his last letter he charged his loved ones at home to be of good heart and fear not. His very last words were: 'I am in God's hands'. Here was the courage and faith of a brave and good man. The tears which come to us, unbidden, must be for ourselves. They cannot be for him whose whole life piled up that great, wonderful, accumulative trust.

On 10 July, only five days after Bell's heroic attack on the machine gun, he and the rest of the battalion were defending the village of Contalmaison, which had just been captured from the Germans. Early in the evening German forces mounted a strong counter-attack. The 8th Green Howards (sister battalion to the 9th) mounted a defence, hastily throwing up a barricade, but nevertheless found themselves hard-pressed. Bell and a number of other skilled bombers from the 9th were sent in to assist them.

Upon arriving at the scene, Bell immediately displayed the same kind of courage and lack of regard for his personal safety that he had a few days previously. He led his party of bombers beyond the barricade and dashed forward to attack the enemy. One of his fellow officers witnessed the moment this fine man was brought down:

Bell dashed forward with an armful of bombs, and started to clear out a hornet's nest of Huns who were ready to take toll of our advancing troops. He advanced with great courage right up to where the enemy were posted. He took careful aim and bowled out several of the Germans. Unfortunately he was hit . . . for a while he fought on, but was hit again. He got weaker and weaker, and had to relax his efforts. He collapsed suddenly and when we reached him he was dead.

It is fitting that Bell lost his life in so brave and glorious a manner, but a terrible tragedy that he had to die at all. That self-deprecating letter he wrote to his mother was the last communication he ever sent home. It must have reached his family at approximately the same time as the news of his death.

Bell died unaware that his gallantry had earned him the honour of the Victoria Cross. On 9 September the citation for this was published in the *London Gazette*:

For most conspicuous bravery. During an attack a very heavy enfilade fire was opened on the attacking company by a hostile machine gun. 2nd Lt. Bell immediately, and on his own initiative, crept up a communication trench and then, followed by Corpl. Colwill and Pte. Batey, rushed across the open under very heavy fire and attacked the machine gun, shooting the firer with his revolver, and destroying gun and personnel with bombs. This very brave act saved many lives and ensured the success of the attack. Five days later this very gallant officer lost his life performing a very similar act of bravery.

After the award had been announced Brigadier General T. S. Lambert, the commanding officer of the 69th Infantry Brigade, wrote to Bell's father:

In asking you and all your family to accept our deep sympathy in the loss of your son, may I say how glad we all are to have learnt of the recognition of his life's work given by his Majesty in the award of the V. C. Others will have told you how well he deserved the honour, both in the act which won it, at the capture of Horseshoe Trench, and at Contalmaison, when he lost his life. His was a great example, given at a time when it was most needed, and in his honour the spot where he now lies, and which is now a redoubt, has been officially called 'Bell's Redoubt'. Not only his own battalion but the whole brigade mourned his loss, but his memory will always remain with us while the 69th Brigade or any of its members who fought there remain. It is given to few to stand out among their comrades as he did, but in leading others his life was not given in vain.

There were further expressions of grief and admiration at home, too. On 26 July 1916 the *Harrogate Herald* published a poem dedicated to Bell's memory:

Don

In every straight and many sport, his name
Stood out for honour and unselfishness;
He played the game because it was the game,
Not for his own, but for his side's success.

Simple and single-hearted, strong and clean
Ever the idol of the men he led;
First in the struggle when the field was green,
Foremost in action when the field was red.

His was the upright life that scorns a lie,
His was the post of danger in the van;

Photograph   *Sport and General*

No doubt a percentage of those who watched Saturday's match between Fulham and Clapton Orient are either already in the National Service or about to join it. We do not, therefore, publish the above photograph with any derisive intent. It is still, however, a question whether the continuance of a game which attracts vast crowds of idle lookers-on at a time when tens of thousands of men are dying in their country's cause is decent

An article from the 9 September 1914 issue of *Bystander* magazine questioning the decency of those men who continued to watch and play football a month after the outbreak of war.

Members of the Footballers' Battalion (17th Middlesex) collecting their army pay. Seated on the left is Sir Frederick Wall, Secretary of the Football Association.

Sir George McCrae, founder of McCrae's Battalion (the 16th Royal Scots), into which thirteen members of the Heart of Midlothian squad enlisted in November 1914.

A 1915 recruitment poster for the 17th Middlesex, rebutting a *Frankfurter Zeitung* article which accused the young men of Britain of shirking their patriotic duty by continuing to play competitive football.

A depiction of the 'Christmas Truce' of 1914, as published in the *Illustrated London News*. During this unofficial ceasefire, at several locations on the Western Front German and British troops ventured into no-man's-land, where they exchanged various gifts and souvenirs as well as engaging in impromptu football matches.

Lance Corporal William Angus VC, of Celtic FC and the 8th Royal Scots. Angus played with Celtic from 1911–14, before enlisting on the outbreak of war. In 1915 he earned the Victoria Cross for rescuing a wounded officer whilst under extremely heavy fire, losing an eye and a foot in the process.

A British officer kicks a football towards the German lines to inspire his platoon to charge with him, from *The War Illustrated Album Deluxe*, 1916.

8-inch howitzers firing from the Fricourt-Mametz Valley during the Battle of the Somme, August 1916.

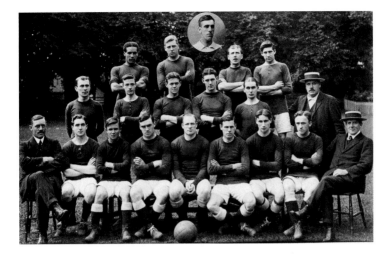

Walter Tull pictured above (back row, far left) in the Northampton Town team of 1912–13, and below with Tottenham Hotspur. Tull was one of the first black footballers to play professionally in England, and the first black combat officer ever to serve in the British army.

Second Lieutenant Donald Simpson Bell VC. Bell played professionally with Bradford (Park Avenue) FC and was commissioned into the 9th Green Howards (Yorkshire Regiment) in 1915. He was awarded the Victoria Cross in 1916 for 'most conspicuous bravery' in leading an assault on a German machine gun post.

William Jonas (front row, with ball) and Richard McFadden (front row, second from right) in the 1914 Clapton Orient team. Both men joined the 17th Middlesex upon the outbreak of war.

The devastated landscape of Delville Wood, 1916. It was here, during the Battle of the Somme, that Jonas bade farewell to his friend and team-mate McFadden before jumping out of the trench they had both become trapped in. He was killed instantly.

Lieutenant Colonel Bernard Vann VC, who played for Northampton Town and Derby County before being commissioned into the 1/8th Sherwood Foresters in 1914. Vann was awarded the Victoria Cross for his 'splendid gallantry and fine leadership' during the Battle of St Quentin Canal, 1918.

His was the death he would have wished to die,
An Englishman – a gentleman – a man.

His now the rest that follows victory won,
The guerdon of the bruised but conquering soul,
His the great Captain's welcome word, 'Well done!'
That crowns the reaching of the Highest Goal.

Finally, Tom Maley, secretary of Bradford Football Club, movingly wrote:

> He played many a fine game for both our teams…A cheery, big chap, he took great interest in his men. He has triumphed, and if blameless life and unselfish and willing sacrifice have the virtue attached with which they are credited, Donald is in the possession of eternal happiness, and in his glorious record and great reward there is much to be envied.

Perhaps all this recognition of her husband's courage and strength of character was some small comfort to Rhoda Bell in the face of a loss that must have seemed so bitterly unfair; the couple had only been married for a little over a month when Donald perished, and they had only spent a handful of days together during that time. On 13 December 1916 she travelled to Buckingham Palace in order to receive the Victoria Cross from the King on Donald's behalf. She received a widow's pension of £100 per annum. She never remarried.

For many years, Donald's Victoria Cross was on display in the Green Howards Museum but it now resides, along with his other medals, at the National Football Museum in Manchester. Although he was buried where he fell, at Bell's Redoubt, in 1920 his remains were reinterred at Gordon Dump Cemetery, Ovillers-la-Boisselle.

Although the men of the 17th Middlesex had been fortunate enough not to have been involved in the initial assaults in the Somme, it was not a state of affairs that could last indefinitely. Two weeks into the battle it had become clear to both sides that a proper breakthrough of their opponent's line was unlikely to be achievable. Both armies therefore turned their attention to capturing whatever tactically significant locations they were able to, in an attempt to gain the upper hand. One such location was Delville Wood, north-east of the village of Longueval, and the British soon began to make a concerted effort to secure it.

The 17th Middlesex began moving towards the front lines on 25 July and eventually relieved the 10th Royal Welsh Fusiliers, taking over custody of some captured German trenches near to the wood. The British artillery had done considerable damage to these trenches prior to the infantry attack that secured them, meaning they offered limited protection and that the ground around them was strewn with unburied corpses – an unpleasant place even by the standards of trench warfare.

On 27 July, following a focused bombardment by the artillery, two battalions – the 1st King's Royal Rifle Corps and the 23rd Royal Fusiliers – attacked the wood early in the morning and were fortunate to find that the guns had smashed German resistance there. With the assistance of other battalions to consolidate positions, by 9 a.m. the wood was secured. As a result a salient was created – Delville Wood now bulged out into the German lines, making holding on to it a far from simple prospect. This point was soon underlined when a retaliatory German bombardment began to pound the wood from three different directions. This was followed by several attacks from German bombing parties. The British troops occupying the woods were overwhelmed and called for assistance; the 17th Middlesex were among the battalions that were moved up in response to this request and began to make their way into the woods in the early afternoon. This was no easy task, as German shellfire was being directed at all the most probable routes in – a deliberate effort to prevent the British from reinforcing. By nightfall, however, several companies of the 17th had made it in. Delville Wood was hardly a wood at all by this point, the whole area churned up by shellfire and many of the trees felled or ablaze. It is easy to imagine why the wood was subsequently given the nickname 'Devil's Wood'.

By the end of the day the 17th Middlesex had suffered significant casualties, including the deaths of two officers and fourteen other ranks. Among that fourteen was Private William Jonas. Born in 1890, Jonas had begun his career with the now extinct club Jarrow Croft before moving to Havanna Rovers. Finally, in June 1912, he transferred to Clapton Orient. He was an extremely versatile footballer and played in many different positions, including goal, though he seems to have preferred forward and midfield. He made a total of 70 appearances for Clapton, during which time he put away 21 goals.

Nobody could accuse Jonas of having had an uneventful time during his time with the club. On one occasion in January 1915 he was sent off for fighting with Millwall goalkeeper Joseph Orme. The indignation this caused among the 16,000 or so fans who were watching the match escalated into a riot, which eventually required the intervention of mounted police.

On top of this, being a handsome young man, Jonas tended to draw the eye of the female fans and received a lot of ardent fan mail. It's hard to imagine that he disliked all this attention but the same probably cannot be said of his wife Mary Jane, whom he had married a few years prior to his move to Clapton. In fact, one of the Clapton Orient programmes eventually had to include the message: 'For the interest of the young ladies of Clapton Park, we have to state that Jonas is married to a very charming young lady.'

Jonas had been among the first players to join the footballers' battalion, along with a number of his Clapton teammates. One of these, Richard McFadden, had been a friend of Jonas's since childhood; it was he who advised Jonas to move to the club in the first place. The two had remained close during their time in the battalion, though while Jonas had remained a private, McFadden had taken up the post of company sergeant major.

During the fighting in Delville Wood the two had

stuck together and found themselves trapped in a trench. While under heavy fire, Jonas decided to make a break for it. Before he leaped out of the trench he turned to McFadden and said simply: 'Goodbye Mac. Best of luck, special love to my sweetheart Mary Jane and best regards to the lads at Orient.' Seconds later handsome Billy Jonas, who was just twenty-six at the time, was mown down before his friend's eyes. Later the Orient goalkeeper Jimmy Hugall said of him:

> He was just the same old Billy out here as he was in the football field, and was liked by everybody. I think he had the heart of a lion and was the life and soul of the Footballers' Battalion. He was one of my best pals, and no one could have wished for a better chum.

For the next two days the men of the 17th Middlesex endured almost incessant artillery fire, punctuated by a series of German attacks with the objective of regaining the wood – or what was left of it. The 17th and the other battalions with them managed to hold out, though at the cost of yet more lost lives. It was only when the 12th Gloucesters and 1st East Surreys managed to push the Germans out of position to the north of the village of

Longueval – which lay on the south-western edge of the wood – that it seemed that further progress was being made, and that Delville Wood might be properly secured. At 9 p.m. on the 29 July the 17th Middlesex were relieved by the 13th Essex and left their positions on the front line. They did so in the knowledge that they had acquitted themselves well and had done all that could have been expected of them. In just those three days of fighting, two officers in the battalion had been killed and eight wounded; thirty-five other ranks had been killed and another 135 wounded.

After only a few days' rest the battalion was moved back into the fighting once more, so that August began with yet more bloodshed, including a second stint in the wood. Then on 8 August they took part in an attack on Guillemont, some distance to the south of Delville Wood. Several attempts to take the village had already failed, and with so many of the battalions in the area suffering from depleted numbers and declining morale as a result of the recent fighting it is perhaps unsurprising that this attack did not go at all well either.

Yet more heavy losses were sustained on that day, among them yet more young footballers. William Gerrish was one such, a promising striker who had started out with Bristol Rovers in 1905 before moving to Aston Villa, where he had a particularly impressive run, scoring against Arsenal in his debut for the club and following this up with a hat-trick against Chelsea. During his time at Villa he won a league medal and also helped the club to move up into the First Division. He transferred to Preston North End in 1912 but didn't get on well there, almost immediately moving to Chesterfield Town, which is where he was playing before war broke out and he joined the 17th Middlesex. Severe injury to both his legs by shellfire was what brought Gerrish down; he was seen lying on the ground quietly smoking a cigarette as he waited for stretcher-bearers to reach him. He died soon afterwards.

There was also former Manchester United player Oscar Linkson, who went missing in action, never to be seen again. Allen Foster, who played for Reading, died in a casualty clearing station after being felled by machine-gun fire. Lastly, Clapton Orient's George Scott was badly injured and captured by the Germans, only to die of his wounds a few days later.

Over the next couple of days the beleaguered 17th Middlesex suffered casualty after casualty in the fighting around Guillemont. However unpleasant the first few months of the war had been in comparison to home, it was nothing to the wholesale slaughter that was happening up and down the Somme valley, and which they now found themselves a part of. The 17th Middlesex suffered 500 casualties or more over this brief period. The battalion was left an exhausted, bloodied shadow of its former fighting strength.

It is in the middle of these dark days – when the Allied loss of life was on a scale previously unimagined, and yet for Haig and the other commanders there seemed no option but to continue sending yet more to their deaths – that we pick up the story of maverick Welsh goalkeeper Leigh Roose once more. As mentioned previously (see page 81), since they had no evidence to the contrary his family had been forced to accept that he had lost his life in the final days of the Gallipoli campaign. However, in his remarkable book *Lost in France*, Spencer Vignes reveals that this was not, in fact, the case.

It was a chance conversation that Helena Jenkins (Roose's sister) and her husband John had after the war, in 1920, with the *Daily Mail* sports cartoonist Tom Webster that made the family realise they did not have the complete story. Helena's son Dick, who was also present, explained to Vignes:

At some point one of us, I can't remember who, said how sad it was about what had happened to Leigh at Gallipoli and how much he would have enjoyed an occasion like this. And straight away Tom said, 'No, he didn't go missing at Gallipoli. I played cricket with him in Egypt after the evacuation.' That was the moment that we realized he had managed to get out.

Naturally the family did everything they could to find out what could have happened to Roose, writing to everyone they could think of who might possibly have information. Their research did bear out what Webster had told them, as several people had had chance meetings with Roose after Gallipoli, including in France in 1916. Finally, from a letter Roose had sent to his friend George Holley it became apparent that he had joined the 9th Royal Fusiliers and would therefore have been fighting in the Somme with them. This new information was obviously a huge leap forward, but then their investigations were confounded – when they contacted the Royal Fusiliers to discover what, in the end, had happened to Leigh they were told unequivocally that, according to the records of the regiment, no man called Roose had ever served with the regiment. Helena Jenkins died without ever finding out what really happened to her brother.

We can now be sure that he did indeed join the Royal Fusiliers, and we also know the reason that he could not be found in the records. It was a simple case of misspelling: in 1916 one L. Rouse enlisted as a private in the regiment. While one might speculate that Leigh had deliberately decided to enter under an assumed name for some personal reason, such as to hide from something or someone, the name is so close to his own that this seems a rather far-fetched explanation. If he had wished to disguise his identity, it is surely much more probable that he would have changed his name entirely. As it is, it seems safe to assume that this was just a mistake during the recruitment process – nothing more than a clerical error.

This does clarify what Roose's movements must have been in the middle of 1916. Clearly he had decided, following Gallipoli, that he wanted to actually fight in the war rather than just provide medical care to those who did – however essential and admirable this service might be. He had therefore left the Royal Army Medical Corps in order to take up a position with the Fusiliers in July. With the French close to buckling under the weight of the German assault at Verdun and the British throwing themselves into the vast offensive on the Somme, and given that he already had real war experience, it is unsurprising that Roose – or Rouse – found himself sent out to France almost immediately.

As we have seen from the experiences of the men of the 17th Middlesex and 16th Royal Scots, reinforcements were soon desperately needed on the Somme, and Roose became one of the many soldiers sent to replenish the dreadfully thinned ranks of the battalions there. Once he joined up with the 9th Royal Fusiliers he saw his first action in the first week of August, in the area around the village of Pozières where the Royal Fusiliers were fighting hard to gain ground from the Germans. They had already succeeded in capturing a couple of German trenches and were intent on taking another known as 'Ration Trench'. They succeeded in doing so with a night attack on 4 August. However, they then found themselves on the receiving end of a concerted counter-attack by the Germans.

Some of the German troops who attacked that night did so armed with one of the new weapons they had deployed in the war: the *flammenwerfers,* or flame-throwers. These utilised a tank of fuel oil carried on the back; the flammable oil was then expelled from a hose using pressurised nitrogen and ignited as it left the firing tube. It is not difficult to understand why these were a much-feared addition to the German arsenal – there can be few deaths more terrible than being burned alive.

Roose's response to the German advance is recorded in the Royal Fusiliers' regimental history, though naturally with his name spelled incorrectly:

> Private Leigh Rouse, who had never visited the trenches before, was in the sap when the *flammenwerfer* attack began. He managed to get back along the trench and, though nearly choked with fumes with his clothes burnt, refused to go to the dressing station. He continued to throw bombs until his arm gave out, and then, joining the covering party, used his rifle with great effect.

Leigh's powerful throws obviously made their mark, just as they had on football pitches up and down Britain in happier times. He and his comrades managed to see off the German attack and barely conceded any ground in the process. For his remarkable steadfastness in the face of such a frightening weapon of war, Leigh was subsequently awarded the Military Medal.

From then on Leigh's life was that which we have by now become familiar with for a British Tommy:

constant rotation in and out of the trenches, periods of constant danger interspersed with periods of brief respite. He did distinguish himself once more, this time by achieving advancement to the rank of lance corporal. Meanwhile the Somme offensive wore on throughout the summer, with both sides battering each other for all they were worth without either one gaining any conclusive advantage. The landscape was strewn with bodies. Summer became autumn and weather conditions worsened. The bodies of the fallen began to be swallowed by mud. The end of another year of campaigning was approaching.

We do not know the exact circumstances under which the indomitable, idiosyncratic Leigh Roose finally laid down his life, but we are able to pinpoint the occasion on which his death occurred. On 7 October 1916 the 9th Royal Fusiliers were part of an attack that had as its objective a portion of the German defences named 'Bayonet Trench'. The attack had already been delayed by forty-eight hours due to the abysmal weather. When we consider this, along with the fact that the artillery of both sides had been firing upon the opposing lines for some time, it's easy to imagine what a dreadful state the landscape must have been in, not to mention the men themselves.

The British attack took place just after 1.30 p.m. It was a complete failure. Not only did it prove impossible to dislodge the Germans from Bayonet Trench, but in some parts of the line the Fusiliers actually came close to losing ground. Leigh Roose was last seen charging in the direction of the German line and he was not amongst those of the 9th Royal Fusiliers who made it back that night. Somewhere out in the confusion, a German shell or bullet brought him down. His body was never found, but at least now we know that the L. Rouse who is commemorated on the Thiepval Memorial is none other than Leigh Roose, Prince of Goalkeepers.

Both the 17th Middlesex and the 16th Royal Scots were reinforced with newer recruits just as the 9th Royal Fusiliers had been by the addition of the draft that had included Leigh Roose. Once bolstered in this way, both battalions took part in further significant operations, doing the best they could under appalling conditions: attacking when ordered, resting when they were able. These were the months when they all truly learned the miserable, prolonged and remorseless nature of the conflict of which they were a part.

Even those fortunate enough not to have lost their

lives out on the battlefield might never be the same again. In the case of some of the footballers, many of them had been so severely wounded that they would never be able to play at a decent level again. Lance Corporal Alfred Taylor, who had played outside left for Brighton & Hove Albion, suffered severe injuries to his shoulder and his leg; Private Fred Keenor of Cardiff City irreparable damage to his knee and Millwall's Jack Borthwick to his skull. Patrick Crossan of Heart of Midlothian – the good-looking player who purportedly could 'pass anything but a mirror' – was struck in the left leg by shrapnel. In the field hospital he was recommended for amputation, though in the end he avoided this, his foot saved by a captured German surgeon. All these men would live, but it was highly unlikely that any would ever play in a league match again.

Moreover, later in the year ill health took Colonel Sir George McCrae out of action and away from the 16th Royal Scots. McCrae was by now fifty-six years old and the burden of command was clearly weighing heavily upon him. He was run-down and had lost a significant amount of weight. With regret he decided that it was time to step aside. On 25 November 1916 the battalion assembled to bid him farewell and a car arrived to take him to the station. Arthur Stephenson would take over command in his stead. It was the end of thirty-eight years of military service for McCrae, and losing their eponymous leader, the man who had started it all, must have been a blow to the men in his battalion.

Physical illness and injury were not the only threats to wellbeing. Many men were exhibiting symptoms of psychological trauma, or 'shell shock' as it was termed. The constant fear and pressure that soldiers lived under – and the emotional distress they suffered as a result of the violent acts they were, of necessity, forced to commit or witness on fellow human beings – were starting to take their toll. Symptoms ranged from anxiety and amnesia to ticks, tremors, pains and hallucinations. Although it was accepted that the condition amounted to more than simple cowardice on the part of the sufferer, the causes were still poorly understood. The best that could be offered to most of these men once a diagnosis had been made was rest and quiet wherever possible.

Among those who were brought to their psychological breaking point was the 17th Middlesex's company sergeant major, Tommy Gibson, who was a former captain of Nottingham Forest. Given the fact that one of the traumas he suffered was being buried alive by a shell explosion, his condition is hardly surprising.

Even leaving aside extreme cases of psychological hurt, the general morale of the troops had sunk to a real low. How could it not have done – as 1916 began to draw to a close, the men of the British Expeditionary Force had spent half a year witnessing friends and comrades falling in action after action around the numerous woods and villages of the Somme valley, with barely any gains to show for it. The last significant attack of the Battle of the Somme was the Battle of Ancre, which concluded on 18 November 1916. By that time, having started their offensive on 1 July, the British and French had advanced just six miles on a sixteen-mile section of the front. That small amount of progress had been achieved at the cost of a staggering 485,000 British and French casualties, a figure that includes 72,191 men whose bodies were never recovered from the battlefield – it is they who are commemorated on the Thiepval Memorial of which there has been cause to mention so frequently in this chapter. That memorial can be seen for miles, and stands as a stark reminder of one of the worst battles that the British army has ever been involved in – before or since.

Of course it wasn't only the British and French who suffered. The Germans had sustained an even more appalling 630,000 casualties. For all concerned, 'the Somme' would become synonymous with death and bloodshed. As the German officer Friedrich Steinbrecher said, 'Somme, the whole history of the world cannot contain a more ghastly word.'

The ramifications of the battle would be felt for more than a generation in Britain, not least because it was the first conflict in which large numbers of Kitchener's Army (those who had answered the call for volunteers since the beginning of the war) had seen serious action. Men who had formerly been civilians were dying in their droves, and the impact on communities back home was heightened by the well-meaning innovation of pals battalions. While it might have seemed a comforting and attractive prospect to go off to war with the guarantee that you would be fighting side-by-side with the men you had chosen to join up with, in practice it meant that whole villages and communities were losing the majority of their young men at a stroke.

Field Marshal Haig already had plenty of detractors by this point, among them the future prime minister, Winston Churchill, but he was also a personal friend of the King's, meaning his position as commander-in-chief was secure. In spite of the prevailing feeling of failure and deplorable losses, Haig argued that the campaign in 1916 had been a success. In his official dispatch from the front in December he insisted that: 'Verdun had been relieved; the main German forces had been held on the Western front; and the enemy's strength had been very considerably worn down. Any one of these three results is in itself sufficient to justify the Somme battle.'

A meeting of the Allied commanders in Chantilly at the end of November affirmed this view. In spite of the lack of a breakthrough on the Somme, the overall tactical situation was felt to be positive, with success of the Russian campaigns in the east having forced Germany to transfer forces to support their beleaguered Austro-Hungarian allies. It was therefore agreed that it was essential to press on with further sustained assaults the following year, in order to stretch the enemy's resources to the limits. Do that, it was thought, and victory would soon be achieved.

8

Another Year

Until now we have not mentioned perhaps the most remarkable of all the men who served with the 17th Middlesex – Walter Tull. Walter was born in Folkestone, on 28 April 1888, to Alice Palmer, a local girl from a family of farm labourers, and Daniel Tull, a Bajan carpenter born into a family of slaves in the Caribbean.

Daniel Tull had left Barbados when he was twenty, having taken a job as a joiner on a ship bound for England in the summer of 1876. Although he had been born after the Slavery Abolition Act of 1833, the standard of living for emancipated slaves in the British colonies remained extremely poor for many years after the act was passed, with opportunities for work often limited to chronically underpaid apprenticeships. Upon arriving in Folkestone, therefore, Daniel had decided to stay, finding work as a carpenter.

Walter had two brothers, William and Edward, and two sisters, Cecillia and Elsie. The whole family lived at 51 Walton Road, and though living conditions were fairly cramped, with the boys sharing one bed and the girls another, the family were otherwise content and seemingly encountered remarkably little prejudice, in spite of how rare interracial families were at the time.

Tragedy beset the Tulls in 1895, however, when Alice died of breast cancer. Walter was just seven at the time. Since Daniel was struggling to care for the family on his own, Alice's niece Clara came to help. Spending so much time together, she and Daniel evidently grew close, and married the following year. But the marriage was to be short-lived, as Daniel fell ill with heart disease and died on the 11 December 1897. The Tull children suddenly found themselves orphans. With nowhere else for them to go, Walter and his brother Edward, by now aged nine and eleven respectively, were sent to Dr Stephenson's Children's Home and Orphanage on Bonner Road in Bethnal Green, East London.

Walter's athletic abilities were immediately spotted by his teachers at the orphanage and he quickly made a name for himself on the football team; Edward, more musically inclined, joined the choir. Their individual talents would unfortunately lead to separation when, in 1900, Edward was adopted by a Glaswegian family who had been struck by the beauty of his voice when the orphanage choir was passing through on a fundraising tour. Walter remained in London, but maintained a relationship with his brother, travelling to visit him in Glasgow on several occasions. The father in Edward's adoptive family was a dentist, and when Edward later went into the same profession he became the first black dentist in Britain.

Luckily, Walter's talents on the playing field eventually gave him a route out of the orphanage too, and in 1908 he was invited for a trial at the local amateur club, Clapton. On joining them, Walter immediately proved his worth and went on to become Clapton's star centre forward, helping to win them three competitions in the 1908–09 season: the FA Amateur Cup, the London Senior Cup and the London County Amateur Cup.

Such achievements did not go unnoticed by bigger teams and in 1909 Walter signed with Tottenham Hotspur, thus becoming only the third person of Afro-Caribbean or mixed heritage to play professional football in the UK, and the first to play in an outfield position in the top division of English football. At his new club, Walter earned £4 a week – around £400 in today's money – which was the maximum wage for a professional footballer at the time and a far cry from the poverty of his youth. The game also took him to parts of the world which must previously have seemed so far-flung that he would never even have contemplated the possibility of visiting them. In the summer of 1909, Walter went on Tottenham's close-season tour of Argentina and Uruguay, during which he scored in a 2-2 draw with Everton and was mentioned in the *Buenos Aires Herald*, who reported that, 'early in the tour Tull has installed himself as favourite with the crowd'.

Unfortunately, Walter's career at Spurs was marred by occasional incidents of racist abuse. During a game at Bristol City on 2 October 1909, Walter was on the receiving end of chants from the home crowd that were described in the *Football Star* newspaper as 'lower than Billingsgate' (a reference to the notoriously foul-mouthed traders in London's Billingsgate Fish Market). The same report went on to say:

> Let me tell these Bristol hooligans (there were but few of them in a crowd of nearly twenty thousand)

that Tull is so clean in mind and method as to be a model for all white men who play football whether they be amateur or professional. In point of ability, if not in actual achievement, Tull was the best forward on the field.

In an attempt to shield him from abuse, Walter was dropped to the reserves by Tottenham. He stayed there for the majority of the 1910–11 season, making only three further appearances for the first team.

Though this must have been an incredibly frustrating experience for so young and ambitious a footballer, it was not to remain the case for long. In October 1911, the legendary Arsenal manager and former Spurs player Herbert Chapman, who was in charge at Northampton Town, was in need of a new centre forward for the team. Through his old friends at Tottenham, Chapman came to hear of a certain talented young player languishing in the reserve team. He invited Walter for a trial at Northampton, and Walter made an instant impression. Newspapers at the time reported that a subsequent deal between the two teams was concluded for 'a heavy transfer fee'. Walter was the first black or mixed-race man to play for Northampton Town, just as he had been the first for Tottenham, but this time he did not encounter the same kind of abuse that had previously all but scuppered his career. He went on to make 111 appearances for the Cobblers before the outbreak of war.

On 21 December 1914, in response to the call for Britain's footballers to set an example to the rest of the country, Walter dutifully enlisted in the 17th Middlesex, the first Northampton Town player to do so. He spent the next year in training with the rest of the battalion, earning three promotions in the process, and by the time the battalion was sent to northern France towards the end of 1915, he was a lance sergeant.

As we have seen, although the 17th Middlesex's first experience of the Western Front did not see them immediately engaged in serious fighting, it was by no means uneventful. The first three months of 1916 were split between training and providing relief for other Allied regiments, with most of the action encountered by the battalion taking the form of bombardment from German rifle grenades and trench mortars. Towards the end of April, when the 17th took up position on the front line near Calonne, the Germans launched an extremely fierce campaign of artillery bombardment against the waterlogged trenches in which the members of the battalion were holed up.

This went on for three sleepless days and nights before the enemy changed their tack and released a mixture of chlorine and phosgene gases from a position to the left of the 17th. Although this particular combination was a relatively new form of chemical weapon, and had potentially even worse effects than chlorine alone, all Allied soldiers were now issued with 'PH' helmets (an early type of gas mask), which offered a good degree of protection.

This would have been Walter's first taste of the terrors of war, and more shelling, gas attacks and machine-gun fire followed over the next few days. The constant scream of artillery shells and the terrible conditions in the trenches began to take their toll on the men. Walter was among the first to fall victim to the effects of shell shock; on 9 May, having been diagnosed as suffering from 'acute mania', Walter was sent back to England to recover. As such he was lucky enough to avoid the opening months of the Somme campaign in which so many lost their lives.

He spent the next few months recuperating in hospital, before being declared fit to return to action. When he did so on 20 September, he was posted not to the 17th Middlesex but to the 23rd Middlesex. This had been raised as a second footballers' battalion on

29 June 1915, not long after the 17th had left to begin training. Once again it was Joynson-Hicks who was the driving force behind it, evidently pleased with the response when the call for men for the 17th had gone out. It was with the 23rd Middlesex that Walter went on to fight on the Somme.

Walter returned to the front line with the second footballers' battalion during the Battle of Flers–Courcelette, which is primarily known for being the battle in which the British army employed tanks for the first time. During the course of Flers–Courcelette, and also Le Transloy (part of the final offensive on the Somme), the 23rd Middlesex suffered terrible losses. In spite of this, Walter demonstrated remarkable courage and he emerged at the end of the year with a recommendation for a commission, signed by Lieutenant Colonel Alan Haig-Brown – himself also a former Tottenham player.

Given that he had previously suffered psychological trauma serious enough for him to be invalided home, it is surely all the more impressive that Walter should have rallied to conduct himself so admirably during his second stint in combat. What is even more astounding is that Walter was recommended for a commission in spite of the fact that, at the time, army regulations did not allow such an appointment on the grounds of his ethnicity. The manual of military law at the time explicitly stated that 'aliens, negroes, etc.' were only able to enlist in the armed forces provided that:

> the number of aliens serving together at any one time in any corps of the regular forces shall not exceed the proportion of one alien to every fifty British subjects, and that an alien so enlisted shall not be capable of holding any higher rank in His Majesty's regular forces than that of a warrant officer or non-commissioned officer.

Appalling as it may seem, this clause meant that even though Walter was a British citizen by birth, for him to be commissioned as an officer was forbidden by law. Nonetheless, it seems that his skills and his popularity within the battalion were such that the authorities were willing to overlook the colour of his skin, and on 26 December 1916, Walter returned to England for training as an officer. After a short period of leave spent with his family, he moved to a camp at Gailes in Ayrshire, where he began training with the No. 10 Officer Cadet Battalion.

But though Walter was escaping the cold and

deprivation of a winter on the Western Front for a time, most soldiers had no such luxury. Additionally, although campaigning was drastically reduced, the Allied commanders were keen to continue exerting pressure on the enemy where possible and so small attacks were carried out on some parts of the line. In the main, however, those in charge on both sides were preparing for major actions to come in 1917, desperate to make this the year that they finally exhausted their opponent into submission.

In the first half of 1917 there were a number of occurrences that were of great significance to the course of the conflict. The earliest of these was a German strategic decision on 9 January to adopt a policy of unrestricted submarine warfare. The Germans had in fact been employing U-boats – as they were then known – since the early years of the war. The Royal Navy at the time was the largest and most powerful in the world, and in open naval warfare Germany stood little chance of victory. U-boats, however, allowed them to strike at British ships with relative impunity. At first they had confined their attacks to military targets, but before long they widened their attentions to include British shipping. By 1917 Germany was starting to have difficulties holding out on the Western Front and it was decided to expand this remit still further to include merchant shipping from any nation bringing goods to Britain. It was hoped that in this way they might be able to starve the island nation out of the war. It wasn't a bad plan – Britain was already experiencing shortages of various kinds, and by February was forced to introduce compulsory rationing of essentials such as bread, flour and sugar. On the other hand, it was also a risky plan – America had so far remained neutral in the war, but sinking American vessels might easily change that. However, it was a risk German commanders felt they had to take.

German high command had also settled on another tactical change over the winter months, which they brought into effect on 23 February. On that day, German troops began to execute a carefully orchestrated retreat from the positions they were currently holding to a newly constructed line of strong defensive positions running from Arras to Laffaux. This would come to be known by the Allies as the 'Hindenburg Line' after Paul von Hindenburg, who had just taken over as Chief of the German General Staff; the Germans referred to the fortifications as the 'Siegfried Line'.

Given that 1916 had been a tremendously bloody

year of fighting, and the fact that they had been forced to support their Austro-Hungarian allies against Russia in the east, Germany's resources were now being stretched to their limits. Withdrawing to the Hindenburg Line not only meant that German troops would be fighting from stronger defences, it also reduced the size of the front they had to cover by twenty-five miles so that they were no longer stretched so thinly. The fortifications represented a last – and as the Germans hoped, impenetrable – line of defence that would prevent Allied forces from breaking through into Belgium or Germany.

As they withdrew across France, the German army left a deliberate trail of destruction in their wake to cause as many problems as possible to the Allied advance that they expected would follow them. They burned or booby-trapped abandoned buildings and farmhouses, poisoned water supplies and destroyed roads. It would take weeks for the Allies to be able to attack again in earnest; by relocating, the Germans were forcing them to completely reconsider their strategies.

To make things even more difficult for the Allies, Russia was experiencing domestic problems. The nation was growing sick of the war; they had sustained tremendous losses – casualties were estimated to be as high as 1.8 million by this point. The fact that the Ottoman Empire had declared for the Central Powers meant that one of their major trade routes had been cut off, leading to economic problems. There was a shortage of munitions for troops at the front due to manufacturing issues, and the government's printing of extra money in order to finance the war had led to inflation, which was making life extremely difficult for the poor. Much of the anti-war feeling in the country was focused on Tsar Nicholas II and the rest of the royal family, whose grip on power had been gradually slipping.

In February 1917, Russian workers began a series of strikes and demonstrations in Petrograd (St Petersburg). By 10 March almost all industry in the city had ground to a halt amid protest marches and other political gatherings. The tsar reacted by ordering the army to suppress this public disobedience – by force if necessary – but many of the troops mutinied at this request, refusing to attack their fellow Russians. The city had completely defied the authority of the tsar and he had no way left of enforcing his will. Eventually on 15 March, acting under the advice of some of his remaining ministers, Nicholas II abdicated in an attempt to defuse the situation. He named his brother,

Grand Duke Michael Alexandrovich, as his successor but the duke wisely declined the crown. Nicholas and his family were placed under house arrest.

The following months would see the dismantling of the tsarist autocracy that had ruled Russia for so long. Given the unpopularity of the war among the majority of the Russian people, this change did not bode well for the overall Allied war effort. The other Allied nations rushed to support the new regime in the hope that Russia would not pull out of the war. At the same time, however, Vladimir Lenin was on his way back to Russia after a twelve-year exile in Switzerland. The Germans were hoping that the radical communist and his supporters would seize control of the revolution and pull Russia out of the war, thus freeing up thousands of German troops that could be utilised on the Western Front. For the time being, however, the Russian troops on the Eastern Front fought on.

Almost as if to counter the problems for the Allies on the Eastern Front, on 6 April the United States declared war on Germany. This was in large part a result of Germany's policy of unrestricted submarine warfare and the attacks on American passenger and merchant ships that this had occasioned. In addition, at the end of January British naval intelligence had intercepted and decrypted a telegram from the German foreign secretary, Arthur Zimmermann, to the German ambassador in Mexico City. The so-called 'Zimmermann telegram' promised that Germany would help Mexico recover territory it had lost during the Mexican–American War of 1846–48 in return for Mexico's support in the current conflict. President Woodrow Wilson evidently felt he could no longer turn a blind eye to such activities, and the US Congress supported his request for a declaration of hostilities. Not only would this mean additional troops on the Western Front, but also financial assistance and access to much-needed weaponry and equipment.

With this news to bolster them, on 9 April the Allies began their first major offensive on the Western Front for the year, with an attack at Arras conducted by British, Australian, Kiwi and Canadian forces. It was yet another attempt to break through the German line and transform the stagnant conflict into a mobile war in which the Allied numerical superiority would be telling. It was also designed to draw German attention in order to increase the chances of success of a French assault in the region of Aisne. A large concentration of British forces moved into position, the 17th Middlesex and the 16th Royal Scots among them. On the first day of the attack, which had been preceded by a five-day bombardment, impressive gains were made – most notably by the Canadian Corps, who managed to capture the notorious Vimy Ridge. However, this momentum could not be maintained and once again the hoped-for breakthrough did not materialise, though the Allies continued to push against fortified German positions.

Involved in the fighting around Arras was one man who had probably hoped never to see battle again: Bob 'Pom Pom' Whiting, the former Brighton & Hove Albion goalkeeper. As mentioned earlier in this book, Whiting had gone absent without leave from the 17th Middlesex while invalided home with scabies in 1916 (see page 92). His wife Nellie was pregnant with their third child at the time and it seems likely that Whiting simply could not stand to leave his family and return to the horrors of the Western Front. In doing so he avoided the terrible slaughter of the Battle of the Somme.

Whiting remained absent and free for the greater part of 1916. However, in October he was finally taken into custody and charged with desertion. The arrest was reported in the 21 October edition of the *Brighton Herald*.

HOVE MAGISTRATES COURT
ALBION FOOTBALLER AN ABSENTEE

On Saturday Robert Whiting, a private in the Footballers' Battalion of the Middlesex Regiment, was remanded to await an escort. He was charged with being an absentee since June last, but pleaded not guilty on the grounds that he had been suffering from a complaint for which he entered hospital in May. Defendant told Detective-Sergeant Adlam that he had been treated in hospital, and that he was not in a fit condition to travel. Whiting was before the war the goalkeeper of the Brighton and Hove Football Club, and a very well-known figure in the football world.

Whiting's court martial was held in December 1916 and he was sentenced to nine months' imprisonment with hard labour. However, given the dreadful casualties that had been sustained during the Battle of the Somme and the need for men to replace them, in the new year it was decided that men serving sentences for desertion should be released early in order to be sent to the front. So it was that in March 1917 Bob Whiting went back to the front to join B company of the 17th Middlesex. He was there in time to take part in the summer offensives.

During the early morning of 28 April the footballers' battalion left their trenches and attacked German positions in and around Oppy Wood. It proved to be a terrible day for the 17th Middlesex, who encountered tremendous resistance from the German forces and suffered the single worst day of casualties that they would during the entire war: six officers and 133 other ranks killed and many more wounded. It was a catastrophe for the battalion.

Bob Whiting was among those who were slaughtered that day. Nellie Whiting was informed of his death in a letter from J. G. Howard, the acting adjutant of the 17th Middlesex, sent on 15 May:

> I very much regret to have to inform you that your husband, No. F-74 Private R. Whiting, of this Battalion, was killed in action on the 28th of last month. He was killed instantaneously by shell-fire in the recent offensive operations. Will you please accept my sincere sympathy in your loss.

The commanding officer of the battalion's B company also wrote to Nellie:

> Your husband lost his life while attending to the wounded under fire, and died while doing his duty both well and nobly. He is buried very near the scene of the action near Vimy Ridge.

As did the Reverend Donald Murray, chaplain to the forces:

> Your husband was killed at the post of duty during an attack on the 28th instantaneously by shell fire. It is sad for those left behind but you must remember there is a world to come.

Sadly, because of his previous conviction for absconding, rumours persisted that he had been shot at dawn for attempting to desert once more rather than having been killed in the line of duty. This was obviously tremendously distressing for the widowed Nellie. It was not until after the war that she managed to fully clear her husband's name – with the help of Albert Underwood, secretary of Brighton & Hove Albion, she had the letters of condolence from the 17th Middlesex published by the *Sussex Daily News* on 3 September 1919:

HOW WHITING FELL
DASTARDLY RUMOUR REFUTED

For some time past a dastardly rumour has been in circulation in Brighton to the effect that Whiting, who greatly distinguished himself as a goalkeeper in the service of Brighton and Hove Albion, and previously with Chelsea, was shot as a deserter in France, the real fact being that he fell gallantly in action. Unhappily the rumour has now reached the ears of his widow, and has come as a great shock to her. Fortunately, Mrs. Whiting, who is now living with her fatherless little ones at 3, Albion Square, St. John's Road, Tunbridge Wells, has in her possession official documents and letters which disprove a foul calumny on the heroic dead. These she has forwarded to Mr. Albert Underwood, Secretary of the Albion, with the request that they should be given all possible publicity. They have been shown to a Representative of the *Sussex Daily News*, which gladly opens its columns for the purpose.

Although Bob Whiting was buried close to where he fell, his grave was either lost or destroyed. He is, however, commemorated on the Arras War Memorial. It is to be hoped that history will remember him more for his tremendous footballing talents and the way that he gave his life, rather than for an occasion when simple human frailty made him waver from what his country expected of him.

Also fighting in the Arras area was Alexander 'Sandy' Turnbull. A lance sergeant in the 8th Battalion East Surrey Regiment, he was also a well-known Scottish footballer who had played for both Manchester City and Manchester United.

Turnbull was born on 30 July 1884, in the town of Hurlford in East Ayrshire, a coal-mining community. By the age of sixteen Sandy was working down in the pits helping to support his family – sadly something made all the more necessary by the fact that his father passed away in 1900. Sandy's involvement with Hurlford Thistle, the local amateur side, must have provided some much-needed recreation time. By that time English clubs had cottoned on to the fact there were pools of talent north of the border that it would be beneficial for them to tap. Turnbull's talents soon began to attract attention, and in 1902 Tom Maley, the newly appointed manager of Manchester City, persuaded Turnbull to sign for the club.

It turned out to be the start of a great season for City – to the surprise of the footballing world the club, which had previously been relatively mediocre, fought its way to the 1903 FA Cup final despite having only just been promoted from the Second Division. The match was held at Crystal Palace against Bolton Wanderers. City managed to secure a win by means of a goal from Welsh legend Billy Meredith, and in doing so won themselves their first significant title. It must have been incredibly thrilling for Turnbull, who was only twenty years old at the time.

The following season, young Sandy became top scorer in the league, having put away an impressive twenty goals. City missed out on both the FA Cup and the championship title, the latter in rather regrettable circumstances when things turned ugly during a match against Aston Villa – a match City needed to win in order to secure the championship title. Aston Villa captain Alec Leake was marking Turnbull and became irritated at Sandy's skill in outmanoeuvring him. As a result, Leake lost his temper and threw some mud at Turnbull, who made a rude gesture in response. Leake then threw a punch. The anger Turnbull and his teammates must have felt at this behaviour was no doubt compounded by the fact that City lost this vital game 3-1.

This was only the start of the problems for the team. After the match Leake publicly accused Billy Meredith, Manchester City's captain, of having offered him a bribe if he would help to throw the match. Whatever the truth of this, an FA investigation found against Meredith and he was suspended from playing for a year. In anger at the fact that City did not stand by him and offer him financial support during this period, Meredith blew the whistle on the fact that, in order to secure the best team possible, City had been paying players more than the £4 a week allowed by regulations. Another FA investigation discovered the truth of these allegations and resulted in Tom Maley being suspended from the league for life, while numerous players, including Sandy Turnbull, were suspended until January 1907.

In fact the fractious match against Aston Villa turned out to be the last that Turnbull would play for Manchester City; by the time his suspension period was over he had signed for Manchester United, as had several of his City teammates – even the disgraced Billy Meredith! Acquiring the core of the side that had pulled City so quickly into the limelight turned out to be a stroke of genius on the part of United's manager Ernest Mangnall, and the years that followed saw the club's star rise.

In spite of the issues that had surrounded him Meredith returned to the game in terrific form, and he and Turnbull became an excellent partnership. Meredith sent over the crosses, and Turnbull turned them into goals. United's new team was so effective that they went on to win the 1908 and 1911 championships, as well as the 1909 FA Cup.

The 1907–08 season was a particularly fine one for Turnbull – he scored twenty-five goals in thirty matches, prompting a reporter from the *Manchester Evening News* to write of him: 'A man of big shoulders and quick feet and active brain, "Sandy" is a great player, and a more unselfish inside man I never saw. A great opportunist with class written all over his football.' And the *Manchester Guardian* rhapsodised: 'When Meredith lifts the ball across the goal there are invariably three of his partners in a line ready to receive it and generally it is "Sandy" Turnbull who puts the finishing touch to Meredith's artistry.'

It was just after this season that Turnbull and the rest of the team went on a tour of Austria and Hungary, a tour that had a highly dramatic conclusion. At first everything went well enough, with United easily winning games in Vienna and Budapest (4-0 and 6-2 respectively) and being received amicably by the local fans in spite of the thrashing they gave the home teams. Unfortunately, during a second match in Budapest the home supporters were noticeably more aggressive. During the course of the game, three United players were sent off by the referee. In spite of the tremendous disadvantage this put them at, they still emerged from the match as 7-1 victors. The result prompted all-out rioting from the Hungarian fans, who were only brought under control after a charge by mounted police. The players themselves were pelted with rocks by the angry crowd, injuring several of them.

While this was obviously appalling behaviour, it must be said that Turnbull appears to have had quite a temper himself. On 21 December 1907 he was sent off in a Manchester derby, as the *Manchester Guardian* reported at the time: 'Sandy Turnbull and [Bill] Eadie [Man City's striker] made themselves ridiculous early in the game by repeatedly making grimaces at each other and, in the second half Turnbull lost self-control so far as to strike Dorsett to the ground. He was promptly ordered off the field by the referee.' Turnbull was also disciplined more than once by his club for apparently being 'insubordinate to directors'.

Some of his aggression towards the footballing establishment may have stemmed from Turnbull's feeling that individual players were not always well served by their clubs or by the FA. He had been a member of the Players' Union since its inception on 2 December 1907. One of the things the union was most passionately opposed to was the existence of an upper limit for the wages a footballer could be paid. The FA disliked the union and its agenda so much that in June 1909 it ordered all professional players to leave it or else face being barred from league football. Most players did so, but not Turnbull, nor several of his United teammates; they took to the field wearing Players' Union armbands. Turnbull was temporarily suspended once again, though by Manchester United rather than by the FA.

In spite of these hiccups Sandy's career continued to go extremely well, and the fortunes of Manchester United continued to climb. The first match at the club's new stadium at Old Trafford, which boasted a capacity of 60,000, was played on 19 February 1910. Unfortunately United lost this first game on their new home turf 4-3 to Liverpool, but Turnbull nevertheless distinguished himself by putting away the first-ever goal scored at Old Trafford, which was described by the *Manchester Guardian* a couple of days later: 'Duckworth took a free kick . . . and skilfully dropped the ball some ten yards or more from the goal-mouth. A. Turnbull rushed in with lowered head. The ball was within a foot or two of the ground by the time he got to it, but he met it with that extra-durable head of his and drove it hard into the goal.' Turnbull could not have known how tremendously famous the stadium would one day become, or how many breathtaking goals would be scored there – of which his was the very first.

However, Turnbull's footballing career was to come to a premature end, and not because of the war – it was a match-fixing scandal. On 2 April 1915 Manchester United played Liverpool and it seemed clear that, with the score 2-0 to United, Liverpool were not giving their all. It afterwards came to light that players from both teams had taken bets on the score being 2-0 to United, and that the whole thing had been a set-up. Turnbull was banned for life from the game along with six other players. It is a pity that such a great footballing career had to end in such an unsportsmanlike manner.

But if it was the end of Turnbull's time as a footballer, it was also the beginning of his life as a soldier. With no professional ties to hold him back, and doubtless anxious to escape the opprobrium surrounding the scandal, he enlisted in the 17th Middlesex. He did not, however, end up serving with the battalion in France

– following training he was transferred to the 8th East Surreys as part of a draft on 15 July, and took part in the fighting around Erquinghem-Lys on the Franco-Prussian border.

Turnbull was fortunate enough to endure his first months in the trenches relatively unscathed, in spite of being involved in several dangerous actions. As the year drew to a close, he even found time to put his footballing skills to good use, playing for his battalion team in the Divisional Cup. The 8th East Surreys got off to a flying start in their first match on 5 December against the 8th Battalion Suffolk Regiment, demolishing their opponents 8-0. They followed this up with a convincing 5-2 win against the 10th Battalion Essex Regiment in their next fixture, and a 2-1 win against the team fielded by the 3rd Divisional Supply Column.

This impressive run was enough to get them to the final, which took place on Christmas Day against the Divisional Royal Army Medical Corps. At the end of extra time the score was 1-1 and so it was agreed that a rematch would take place on New Year's Day. This time Turnbull and his teammates managed to do what they had to do, securing a 3-2 victory and giving cause for much celebration.

The win might have been a good start to the year but

the battalion's joy was short-lived; six weeks later they were involved in an attack on Boom Ravine, a strategically important feature of the Somme battlefield. The attack was largely unsuccessful and the battalion suffered 65 casualties. Those losses must have been all the harder for them to bear when the Germans abandoned the position anyway just a couple of weeks later when their withdrawal to the Hindenburg Line began. Along with the rest of the Allied forces, the 8th East Surreys advanced in the wake of the German retreat and eventually, at the start of April, they were moved north in order to participate in the Arras offensive.

Strange as it might seem, on 7 April, just days before the Allied attack was scheduled to begin, the 8th East Surreys football team had to play their first match as defending holders of the Divisional Cup. They saw off their opponents, the team from 18th Division Headquarters, 2-1. Since the 8th East Surreys had not been ordered to take part in the opening actions of the Arras offensive, they were even able to play another match on 9 April, the very day that the attack began. This time they managed only a 1-1 draw against the Divisional Royal Engineers, though they beat them 2-1 in a subsequent replay and then trounced the 7th Battalion East Kent Regiment 4-1 in the semi-final on

12 April. Once again, the 8th East Surreys were in the final of the Divisional Cup. Sandy Turnbull, however, was not destined to play in that match – or indeed any other – as the game was cancelled before it could take place. His battalion were about to move into the front-line trenches.

On 3 May the 8th East Surreys were part of an attempt to capture of the village of Chérisy. Things did not go well from the start. The pre-attack bombardment was neither fierce nor sustained enough to properly break up the enemy's barbed wire, and the German's own artillery offered a fierce reply in return. The infantry assault began at 3.45 a.m., in darkness, making effective communication and informed progress very difficult. Even amid this confusion, some of the battalion did manage to advance to the outskirts of the village. That this was possible at all must largely be due to heroic efforts on the part of individual soldiers, and one who was especially courageous was Sandy Turnbull. The divisional history – *The 18th Division in the Great War* – records that he used a Lewis gun to great effect against enemy machine guns, and carried on fighting in spite of having been hit himself. Eventually, however, he sustained a wound that he could not ignore no matter how determined he was – a bullet in the knee.

Even then he refused to be taken from the battlefield for treatment, instead helping to direct his comrades with a map he was carrying and instructing them to go on without him.

That was the last time that Sandy Turnbull was seen either living or dead. The 8th East Surreys were later forced to retreat from their objective. It was initially thought that he might have been captured by the Germans, but sadly this proved not to be the case. Most likely, Turnbull was left behind on the battlefield to bleed out from his wounds.

There may be a few unfortunate incidents that stain the record of Sandy Turnbull's footballing career. Nevertheless he was an extraordinarily talented player, and those occasional errors of judgement are surely eclipsed by the courage with which he conducted himself in the final hours of his life. As the divisional history notes: 'He was a gallant man, and met a soldier's end with calm fearlessness.' It seems that the footballing authorities agreed, posthumously pardoning him for the match-fixing affair in 1919.

9

Passchendaele

In spite of the concerted efforts made by the Allies, the summer campaigns of 1917 were still not yielding the hoped-for results. Significant territorial gains had been made in the early stages of the Arras offensive, which had also succeeded in its objective of drawing the German forces away from the Aisne sector and thereby maximising the chances of success for the Nivelle Offensive that began on 16 April. This French attack had been planned as the main event of the Allied summer strategy, meant to decisively break the German line in less than forty-eight hours. It failed to do so and, to make matters worse, the French troops began to mutiny, provoked no doubt by the tremendous disappointment that the offensive had become just another bloodbath rather than being the action to end the war that many had hoped.

The mutinies began with the 2nd Division when they refused to follow orders to attack on 3 May. Various other divisions and regiments followed, staging protests and electing men to speak on their behalf in order to demand an end to the offensive, which was indeed suspended as a result on 9 May. The mutinies were only checked when the French commander-in-chief Robert Nivelle, who had masterminded the attack, was ousted and replaced with Philippe Pétain. Pétain swiftly executed a small number of mutineers as an example, while commuting this sentence for the vast majority who were convicted and promising that there would be no more major offences of the sort that had just been carried out until the American army arrived at the front.

It was obvious that French morale hung by a thread and that to push things further could mean losing the war. While order might have been restored in the ranks of the French army for the time being, there was no telling what might happen if they suffered any more heavy losses or if the troops felt themselves poorly treated. The Allied strategy for the year had to be reconsidered at once.

Since the beginning of 1916, British commanders had been keen to break through Flanders and reach the Belgian coast – they wanted to gain control of the ports there in order to stop them from being used as staging grounds from which to attack vital shipping. However, as 1916 had been the year of both the ferocious German attack on Verdun and the terrible bloodshed on the Somme, any ambitions they had in this direction had necessarily been shelved. Now, the weakened, mutinous condition of the French army in the Aisne sector meant that undertaking an offensive that would draw German forces away from them suddenly became much more attractive, even necessary.

It had long been thought that the best starting point would be the capture of Messines Ridge. The ridge was part of the high ground to the south of Ypres and provided advantageous views of the surrounding countryside. From it, the next objective would be Passchendaele Ridge, after which the British forces could make their bid for the coast. This was the plan of attack that Haig finally authorised to be carried out by General Sir Herbert Plumer, who had been preparing for such an action for a year.

A tremendous bombardment preceded the attack, beginning on 21 May and lasting until 2.50 a.m. on

7 June, just before the infantry assault. As if this were not a dramatic enough prelude, engineers had been working for some time to dig beneath the German lines and had constructed numerous mines there. A total of nineteen of these were detonated at 3.10 a.m., all but obliterating the German front lines and killing as many as 10,000 men. After that the Germans were unable to offer much resistance. The British advanced behind a creeping barrage and soon achieved their objectives. It was one of the most efficient operations of the entire war and the German counter-attacks, which continued until 12 June, were unable to regain the ground they had lost.

In fact, so successful was the attack that Haig seems to have become a little overconfident, believing that if Plumer could deliver such results at Messines then it ought to be possible to achieve similar success if they were to push for further objectives in Flanders. However, to continue fighting an offensive campaign while the French army was in such a poor state, and with the first trickle of American forces only just beginning to arrive in Europe, was certainly not an uncontroversial decision. It had some extremely prominent detractors, including Prime Minister Lloyd George and General Foch, French Chief of the General

Staff. Nevertheless, on 25 July Haig received permission from the War Office to press on with his ambitious plan of attack.

The German hold on the area was incredibly strong; they might have lost Messines Ridge but they held the rest of the high ground such as the ridges of Passchendaele and Gheluvelt, giving them an unparalleled view of the plains all around and making it far too easy for them to direct artillery fire. Their positions were also heavily protected – surrounded by barbed wire, machine-gun emplacements and various fortifications. When the poorly drained, artillery-churned condition of the lower ground is also taken into account it becomes hard to imagine worse circumstances for soldiers to fight in.

In spite of all this, the initial attack on Passchendaele, which took place on 31 July after the usual massive bombardment, fared relatively well. Unfortunately for the Allies, however, the weather then betrayed them – by the evening of the first day it was raining hard. It was the start of one of the wettest Augusts in decades, which forced Haig and his commanders to suspend their offensive for the month. One soldier who had to endure the terrible conditions was Walter Tull. He had recently returned from Britain to rejoin the second footballers' battalion, the 23rd Middlesex, having completed his officer-training course with the No. 10 Officer Cadet Battalion. He now wore the single Bath star of a second lieutenant, making him the first black or mixed-race combat officer ever to serve in the British army.

A letter that Walter managed to write to his brother Eddie on 10 August gives some idea of the discomfort that the weather inflicted upon the troops:

On Monday at noon my Coy. Cmndr detailed me to go up and inspect the portion of the trench 'D' Coy were to hold as we were to go up that night. Three other subs and myself started off about 1.30 but Fritz was shelling the back areas like a demon and after dodging about from trench to trench we got fed up and struck across country. We were lucky and got to a tunnel which would help us on our way considerably. Unfortunately the outlet was flooded and we got soaked up to our hips, but H_2O is less dangerous than shrapnel or HE. From the flooded place we had to go along a track knee deep in mud…From there our way lay across open ground formerly no man's land, now one mass of shell holes. It was impossible to proceed in a straight line anywhere of more than one to two yards…Cannot stop to write more now.

A slightly drier September enabled the British to continue with their operations, albeit with a revised 'take and hold' strategy, whereby rather than trying to advance on a wide front they seized a series of smaller strategic objectives and consolidated these positions to ensure they could be held permanently. Although this was a much slower method of advance than had been hoped for, it nevertheless made for continual progress, with key strategic points in the area, such as Polygon Wood and Gheluvelt, being seized. Between 20 and 25 September, Walter Tull and the 23rd Middlesex took part in the fighting around Menin Road Ridge as part of this strategy.

In retrospect it would have been better for the British to stop at this point; after all, they had made significant territorial gains. However, it was decided that they would press on – Haig wanted to take Passchendaele Ridge at the very least. Unfortunately October saw the rain begin again in earnest, once again transforming the battlefield into a sea of cloying mud, strewn with shell holes brimming with stagnant water. Movement and communication were made all but impossible in places, with men even drowning in the slurry of the battlefield. For this reason Passchendaele perhaps encapsulates the typical modern image of all that was hideous about the First World War more than any other battle in the whole conflict.

Given the decision to continue with the offensive in spite of the terrible weather – incidentally Crown Prince Rupprecht of Bavaria, who was commanding the German forces, referred to the rain as 'our most effective ally' in his diary – it is hardly surprising that casualty levels quickly began to climb.

Out there in the freezing mud was a footballer-soldier known for the considerable time that he had spent playing for Blackburn Rovers: Edwin Latheron, commonly known as Eddie. Eddie was born on 22 December 1887 in the North Yorkshire village of Carlin How. He began his career playing in the Northern League, most notably for Grangetown Athletic, close to his home. He cut a diminutive figure, standing at only 5'5", but was easy to spot on account of his red hair, which would later earn him the nickname 'Pinky'. What he lacked in size he evidently made up for in speed and skill, and when a Blackburn Rovers scout attended a match between Grangetown and Blackburn Crosshill in 1906, Eddie immediately caught his eye. Shortly afterwards, Blackburn manager Robert Middleton made him an offer and Eddie made his transition to the big time (Blackburn Rovers was a First Division club).

Given that he was still a teenager, it's not surprising that in his first season he was only fielded in a few games and so didn't have much opportunity to shine. Things improved for him in the 1907–08 season, in which he scored nine goals in twenty-seven appearances, making him the club's joint top goalscorer (along with Billy Davies and Jack Martin). But while this season was certainly progress for Latheron personally, unfortunately the same could not be said for the club: Blackburn were knocked out of both the FA Cup and the Lancashire Cup in the first rounds, and only managed to achieve fourteenth place in the league.

As a reaction to this lacklustre performance a new trainer was engaged by the club – Bob Holmes, who was himself a former player for Preston North End. He succeeded in turning things around for the team, pulling them up to fourth and then third in the league in the following two seasons. Latheron managed to put away ten goals in each. The 1910–11 season saw a slight dip in form for Blackburn, but they bounced back the following year. Despite losing their first two games, they went on an unbeaten run that gave them the momentum they needed to win the league title for the first time in 1912.

By this point Eddie Latheron had become one of

the most important elements of the team and while Rovers finished fifth in 1912–13, with fourteen goals he boasted the distinction of being the club's top scorer yet again. His reliability and skill as a player were clearly coming to wider attention – that year he earned his first international cap when he played for England in a Home International Championship match against Wales on 17 March 1913. Eddie scored one of England's goals, helping to secure a 4-3 win. He made another international appearance against Ireland in February the next year, though this went rather less well, with England losing 3-0. That failure must have been tempered for Latheron by the fact that Rovers managed to come top of the league again in 1914.

At this point in Latheron's career, the war intervened. However, like many footballers he played on for the 1914–15 season, in which Blackburn finished third. He actually continued to play beyond this point, guesting for Blackpool on loan from Rovers for a number of wartime games not endorsed by the FA during 1915–16, and then playing in similar matches for Rovers themselves in 1916–17.

He might have been rather late in joining up – and perhaps it was even the introduction of conscription with the Military Service Act 1916 that eventually compelled him – but Latheron became a gunner for the Royal Field Artillery and was sent to the Western Front, where he found himself caught up in the offensive in Flanders. He was there on 12 October when the Allies made another attempt on Passchendaele in an offensive now known as the First Battle of Passchendaele. The mud made progress incredibly hard and the men were already exhausted and demoralised. The attack was a comprehensive failure.

Two days later, on 14 October, Eddie Latheron was killed by an enemy shell at the age of twenty-nine. More fortunate than many, his body was not lost to the mud; he is buried in a military cemetery at Vlamertinghe, not far from Ypres. His military career may not have been as long or illustrious as that of some of the others discussed in this book, but any man who experienced the almost unparalleled hardships of Passchendaele and laid down his life there nevertheless deserves the greatest respect.

As with the Battle of the Somme, reporting the deaths of the footballers who lost their lives at Passchendaele becomes something of a litany. Fred Griffiths, in contrast to Eddie Latheron, played for quite a number of clubs over the course of his career. A Welshman, he was born in Presteigne on 13 September 1873; his goalkeeping career began in the north of England with stints at various clubs: South Shore, Clitheroe, Blackpool and Stalybridge Rovers. In 1900 he played for Wales in two international matches, one against Scotland and one against England. He was signed to Blackpool at the time, and was in fact the first Blackpool player ever to win an international cap.

Griffiths then moved south to play for a couple of the London clubs, Millwall Athletic and Tottenham Hotspur, but only remained in the capital for a year before he returned to Lancashire to play for Preston North End. Next season he was on the move again, however, taking over as goalie for West Ham United, where he remained for two seasons before joining New Brompton. In 1906 he moved from Brompton to Middlesborough, but here things did not go well and he never made a single appearance for the first team. Griffiths ended his professional career shortly afterwards, going on to play for the minor club Moore's Athletic in Shirebrook, Derbyshire, while also working as a coalminer.

Though his career never attained the dizzy heights of celebrity enjoyed by some of his fellow Welshmen, such as Leigh Roose and Billy Meredith, as a footballer who played for so many different clubs Griffiths was a perfect example of the way that a single player could be remembered fondly by many communities. No longer a footballer by profession, he duly enlisted into the ranks of the 15th Battalion Nottingham and Derbyshire Regiment (also known as the Sherwood Foresters) and rose to the rank of sergeant.

Griffiths and his comrades had actually been in the Somme valley for most of 1917, avoiding the first months of the Flanders campaign. However, in October they were finally moved up to take part in the Passchendaele offensive. Fred was one of four members of the battalion killed in a relatively minor exchange of fire on 30 October. Older than most of the men whose deaths have been mentioned, he was forty-four years old at the time. He is buried at Dozinghem Military Cemetery in West-Vlaanderen, Belgium.

On 10 November the sheer persistence of the British commanders rewarded them with the prize they sought: with the assistance of the Canadian Corps they succeeded in capturing Passchendaele. Although British forces had not managed to gain the Belgian ports, they had successfully diverted Germany's attention and resources from the weakened French forces in the south. The result also seemed, at least to some extent, to be a vindication of the new take and hold tactics they had been deploying. However, once again the casualty rates were appallingly high – some estimates suggest almost a quarter of a million British soldiers were wounded or killed. The figure for Germany is thought to be closer to 400,000. Viewing the battle in retrospect, both sides would later characterise it as a disaster; a General German Staff document commented that 'Germany had been brought near to certain destruction by the Flanders battle of 1917', while Lloyd George wrote later that 'no soldier of any intelligence now defends this senseless campaign'.

Yet this dreadful mud-soaked battle that had all but exhausted both sides was not even the last major action of 1917. Further south, back in France, the Allies had turned their attention to the town of Cambrai, which was being used as a vital supply point for the Hindenburg Line. A large-scale attack was planned, including the use of a large number of Mark IV tanks. This was by no means the first time that tanks had been used in the conflict, but it was felt that the relatively passable chalk landscape around Cambrai would provide a better arena for the armoured vehicles than many of the other battlefields of the war had.

This certainly seemed to be the case at first. On 20

November a combined tank and infantry attack broke the German defences and succeeded in advancing between three and four miles along a six-mile stretch, capturing or destroying 100 enemy guns in the process. However, while this was a great achievement, as many as 179 Allied tanks were out of action by the end of that first day, having been either taken out by the German defences or else broken down. The tanks had opened the attack admirably, but it would not be possible to use them to deliver a second hammer blow to the enemy. There were also some important objectives that had not been captured according to plan, chief among these Bourlon Wood at the north end of the battlefield, close to the tactically desirable Bourlon Ridge.

The second day of the fighting was far from the success of the first day, but Haig nonetheless took the decision to continue with the offensive longer than the forty-eight hours that had originally been set – in spite of the fact that German reinforcements were arriving. Prolonged fighting around Bourlon followed, with each side attacking and counter-attacking with great tenacity.

The 13th East Surreys were one of the battalions in the area and with them was Lieutenant Frederick Wheatcroft. Freddie Wheatcroft was born in Derbyshire in 1882 and began playing for his local football club, Alfreton Town. He was actually a schoolteacher by profession, but this didn't prevent him signing for Derby County in 1903 when his skills as a centre forward were noticed.

Things didn't go particularly well for Wheatcroft there and he was largely overshadowed by striker Steve Bloomer. This is probably the reason that he quickly moved to Swindon Town as an amateur in 1904. However, he returned to Derby a year later for another reasonably undistinguished run, during which he scored four goals in twenty appearances. After turning out for both Fulham and Reading he eventually returned to Swindon in 1909, and remained with the club until the war curtailed his career. It was during this final spell that he played much of his best football; in the 1909–10 season he scored twenty-two goals in thirty-three games, for example.

Wheatcroft first joined the 5th Battalion East Surrey Regiment but later transferred to the 13th as an officer when he received his commission. The 13th East Surreys belonged to the 40th Division, who had succeeded in capturing Bourlon Wood and some parts of Bourlon village itself. On 26 November they were due to be relieved by the 62nd Division in order to allow them some much-needed rest. However, by the time that the order to withdraw came, Wheatcroft and the men with him had advanced ahead of the Allied line and suddenly found themselves cut off. Tanks that were supposed to have supported them never arrived, and the troops that were meant to be providing covering fire had been forced to retreat. Isolated at the edges of the village, they were forced to find whatever cover they could in the remains of houses. It was no use; the machine guns and artillery of the enemy took their toll, cutting down numerous men of the 13th East Surreys – sadly, Freddie Wheatcroft was among them.

As a postscript to this tragic story, though Freddie did not survive the war, Steve Bloomer, his rival at Derby, did. Bloomer had a rather different experience to any of the other players we have mentioned. By the time that war broke out he was already retired; in fact in July 1914 he had moved to Berlin in order to coach the German club Britannia Berlin 1892. Of course this was only a few weeks before the outbreak of war, and shortly after hostilities had been declared Bloomer found himself a resident of Ruhleben, a civilian detention camp just outside the German capital.

With him were a number of other prominent British footballers who had been unlucky enough to find themselves in the wrong country, including two he had played alongside for England, Fred Spiksley and Samuel Wolstenholme. Bloomer and the others remained there for most of the war, and set up their own internal football league – the Ruhleben Football Association – to help pass the time. When Bloomer finally left the camp in March 1918, a special farewell match was staged in his honour.

As 1917 began to draw to a close, so too did the battle of Cambrai. On 3 December Field Marshal Haig ordered a withdrawal from most of the territory that the Allies had gained to more defensible positions. The offensive had, however, managed to demonstrate that the strong fortifications of the Hindenburg Line could be breached – even if they were still yet to be fully – with decisive swift attacks using new infantry and artillery methods and armoured vehicles. The greatest line of German defence was not as impregnable as had been thought.

This might have offered a glimmer of hope, but in light of another year of almost unimaginable losses, for many it must have been cold comfort. It was true that the Allies had held together in the face of numerous difficulties, and that their new tactics had proven much harder for the Germans to counter. It was also true that they now had the support of the United States. However, even if victory seemed possible, many would consider that the price with which it had been bought made it almost no victory at all. Year after year of brutal campaigns – Ypres, the Somme and Passchendaele among them – had robbed so many men of life that they had scarred Britain indelibly.

To illustrate this, take one football club that lost a great many players during 1917, and whose contribution we have yet to recognise: Falkirk. Over the course of the war, seven players from the Scottish club lost their lives in the line of duty. Of these, two had fallen earlier in the war – James Sharp in Flanders on 26 April 1915 and Andrew McCrae in Gallipoli on 17 November 1915. Young James Laing was the next Falkirk lad to die, on 23 April 1917 during the Arras offensive. Laing had been on Falkirk's reserve team and had enlisted into the ranks of the 7th Argyll and Sutherland Highlanders.

Only a few days later, but far away and in completely different circumstances, a fourth Falkirk player fell. Rather than joining the army when the outbreak of war curtailed his football-playing days, John Ramsay had chosen to enlist into the ranks of the Howe Battalion

Royal Naval Division as an able seaman. It was in this capacity that he was killed in action on 28 April 1917 at the age of just twenty. The *Falkirk Herald* reported his death in the 12 May edition, and the story serves to remind us of the many families who had to bear the loss of more than one member during the war:

SECOND SON KILLED

Mrs. Ramsay, 124 Dundas Street, is the recipient of a letter from a naval officer, which states that her son, A. B. J. B. Ramsay, R. N. division, 20 years of age, was on 24th April killed while on active service. The letter reads: 'He was killed in one of the most difficult actions the R. N. D. have ever been in, and he died like a Scotchman. He was a good lad, liked by men and officers alike, willing and obedient. You must be justly proud of your son.' This young sailor was through the Dardanelles campaign, having been a year and nine months on active service, and two years this month with the Navy. He was very well known as a football player for Falkirk, and originally worked in the boatyard.

This is the second son Mrs. Ramsay has lost through the war, another son, Alexander, being also fatally wounded while in action with the R. N. D. some time ago. Another son was discharged through his extreme youth, but expects to be called up again, and her husband is serving in France.

The brother mentioned in the article, Alexander, had been killed in action on 14 November 1916 while serving with Drake Battalion Royal Naval Division. He was only eighteen years old at the time. This author, at least, is able to find no record in the Commonwealth War Graves Commission's records of the third, youngest Ramsay boy losing his life, so it is to be hoped that the war did not deprive Mrs Ramsay of all her children.

On 27 May, Harry Taylor became the fifth Falkirk player to lose his life. Harry was born in 1891 and, being a bit older than the four we have mentioned so far, had played for several clubs before the war. He began his career with Cowie Wanderers in 1910 before moving to Falkirk in 1911. He turned out for Dundee Hibernian in 1912, and then for Stenhousemuir in 1913. At the outbreak of war he had enlisted into the 1/7th Battalion Gordon Highlanders and was killed in action on 27 May 1917 at Rœux.

The sixth from the club who lost his life was the best known – the extremely popular James Conlin. In actual fact he had only played for the club for a brief spell and as he had not done so for years by the time war broke out, it would be much more accurate to say he was a former Falkirk player. As we will see he played for numerous prominent clubs. However, he serves to demonstrate an important fact about all of the footballers who transferred from club to club in their careers: that more than one town therefore felt they had some claim to them, and so a share in the grief when they fell in battle. This further magnified the impact that the deaths of individual players had back in Britain.

James Conlin was born on 6 July 1881 in Consett, County Durham, and grew up to be a fast and agile left-winger. He began his career with the flamboyantly named Captain Colt's Rovers before signing with Falkirk on 9 January 1900, but only remained with them for a season. He joined Albion Rovers in March 1901 and moved yet again in April 1904, this time to Bradford City, with whom he remained for two years, making 67 appearances and scoring ten goals. On 7 April 1906 he represented his country in a Home International Championship match against Scotland, which England won 2-1. His quick reactions and speed on the ball soon had other clubs knocking on Bradford City's door and on 13 July 1906 Conlin moved to Manchester City, where he remained for five successful years before spending a single season at Birmingham.

In 1912 he moved back to Scotland in order to play for Airdrieonians. By this time, however, Conlin was suffering from problems with alcohol and his time there was not all that might have been hoped for – he even failed to turn up to a match on one occasion. He and the club soon parted company and on 13 August 1913 he made his final transfer, this time to Broxburn Athletic. This was to be the last club he ever played with in his considerable football career.

Conlin eventually enlisted into the 15th Battalion Highland Light Infantry. He was with them when they transferred to the Nieuwpoort sector on the Belgian coast in June 1917, in readiness to support the British offensive at Passchendaele. It was here that he died, leaving behind his wife Elizabeth and their two small children. A small obituary appeared in the *Falkirk Mail* on 15 September 1917:

FORMER FALKIRK FOOTBALLER KILLED

Mrs Conlin, Coatbank St, Coatbridge, has received a letter telling her of the death in action, on 24th June, of her husband Pte. James Conlin. H. L. I. Pte.

Conlin was a well-known sportsman and for some time played with Falkirk Club. It was with Albion Rovers, however, that he attained fame and thereafter played with Bradford City. He was capped twice for England in one season in the Association and League Internationals against Scotland. He was also at one time in the Manchester and Birmingham elevens. On his return to Scotland he played with Airdrie for one season.

We can imagine similar notices in local papers in all the towns that had known and accepted Conlin as one of their own.

The last player associated with Falkirk who fell was Alexander Brown Johnston, who had turned out for the club between 1904 and 1906. He was killed in action while serving as an acting bombardier in the Royal Garrison Artillery. A further fifteen Falkirk players had joined the colours in various capacities and participated in the war. Many of them were wounded or else suffered shell shock. Several were so badly affected by their experiences that they never fully recovered.

If considered individually, the lives and deaths of each of these men who had represented Falkirk at one time or another are perhaps not remarkable – at least in the context of a war that was reducing great swathes of the population to mere casualty figures – but collectively they demonstrate the real human impact that the mounting losses had on individual towns. The war was hollowing out institutions and communities, leaving empty spaces where before there had been fit young men. By this point, nowhere in Britain remained untouched by such losses. Of course it was not just footballers – every profession and every social stratum was affected – but the visibility of the players, and the esteem in which they were held by so many communities, is a clear reminder of this stark reality.

To make matters worse, as 1917 drew to a close Russia pulled out of the war, negotiating a ceasefire with the Central Powers. For most of the year three separate groups had struggled for control of the country. In the end it was the most radical of these, Lenin's Bolsheviks, who managed to seize power on 6 November. Shortly after this, on 26 November, Russia called for a general end to hostilities, which the Allies failed to respond to. When they continued to ignore such communications, Russia began to make peace arrangements of its own; on 15 December, a ceasefire was declared on the Eastern Front. To negotiate a proper peace treaty would take several months more and would prove a complicated affair, but to all intents and purposes Russia was now out of the war.

While it was certainly understandable that Russia, which had suffered so much civil unrest, would want an end to the conflict, they would pay dearly for doing so. They had lost a great deal of land to the advancing armies of the Central Powers, including Finland, Poland, Latvia, Ukraine and Belarus. And, Russia's national concerns aside, this was a far from welcome development for the Allies, as it freed up a great many enemy troops to make their way now from the Eastern to the Western Front.

If the war were not won soon, would anyone even recognise the Britain that was left?

10

The Bloody Road Home

With Russia out of the picture, the Germans quickly gained a numerical advantage against the Allies. By spring 1918 they had 192 divisions on the Western Front, in contrast to 155 French and British combined. The German commanders were also keenly aware that the full weight of the American military would be arriving on the continent imminently. Once that happened, securing a victory would be all but impossible. If Germany were to have any chance of winning the war, General Erich Ludendorff, Haig's opposite number, had to strike decisively before the American Expeditionary Forces became involved.

Haig and the other Allied generals were keenly aware

of this, and also concerned about the weakened state of the British forces after the bloody campaigns of 1917. There were enough soldiers in Britain to provide the necessary reinforcements, but the War Cabinet was far from keen on the idea. Battles such as Passchendaele had seemed to demonstrate that if Haig had the men available he would not hesitate to use – and lose – them. As far as Lloyd George and his colleagues were concerned, it would be far better to wait until the United States arrived on the scene before committing a great many more troops.

The War Cabinet did, however, sanction the reinforcement of depleted units through the breaking up and personnel reassignment of other units. But it was hardly an answer to the request for more men; effectively it amounted to a structural consolidation of the forces already out in Belgium and France. Brigades from most divisions were reduced from four battalions to three, and the surplus men reassigned elsewhere. It is here that the story of one of the original footballers' battalions comes to an end: the 17th Battalion Middlesex Regiment was one of the 115 battalions selected for complete disbandment.

The 17th Middlesex had seen a great deal of action in 1917, taking part in both the Arras and Cambrai offensives. In truth, few of those who had enlisted at the founding of the battalion were left, and there were only around thirty footballers remaining. Still, it was a hard blow for the men when they were informed on 3 February 1918 of their impending disbandment. They were no longer the optimistic bunch of pals who had signed up after that first patriotic meeting in Fulham – a day that must have seemed far distant to the few that could remember it – but the battalion had provided a sense of belonging and constancy, even as they lost comrades and former teammates in the grim routine of battle.

On the night of 6 February, the 17th Middlesex were in support trenches near Villers-Plouich, a village south-west of Cambrai, when they were relieved of their posts for the last time and sent to billets prior to being reassigned. It was the final chapter in the story of a battalion that had initially been notable for its famous members, but which had distinguished itself with an exemplary service record. Lieutenant Colonel Stafford later wrote: 'At the final parade of the battalion, I said that . . . I should never be so proud of anything as having commanded the Footballers' Battalion'.

Having thus reorganised itself, the British Expeditionary Force – stretched dangerously thin by lack of manpower – could only wait for Germany's move. When it came on 21 March, it was more swift and terrible than anyone could have feared.

General Ludendorff had decided to target the British forces rather than the French, planning a massive northwesterly assault to drive the British back towards the sea and, in doing so, seize control of the Channel ports that were so essential for their supply lines. It was a vast and ambitious undertaking, and more than anything it needed to happen quickly – Germany could not afford for the attack to stall once more into the slow grind of trench warfare.

Rather than a prolonged period of artillery attack, like that which had heralded the beginning of so many other campaigns, Ludendorff began his assault – 'Operation Michael' – with a short, intense bombardment lasting only five hours. Given that it was carried out with well over 6,000 guns and focused with deadly accuracy on key targets from HQs to supply lines, it was no less hellish for its relative brevity. They fired more than one million shells in that short time – not far off the total the Allies had fired during a whole week in their great assault on the Somme in 1916. This was followed up with a tremendous infantry attack along more than forty miles of the British line. The German army employed units of 'storm troops', who used infiltration tactics to bypass heavy defences and disrupt enemy communication lines and artillery units.

The British army was forced to pull back in the face of this blistering assault. It seemed that nothing was able to stem the relentless German advance, and by the end of the first day British casualties were already at 50,000. The assault had broken through in more than one place on the section of the line defended by the British Fifth Army. Within two days, the Fifth Army was forced into full retreat.

On the second day of the assault yet another footballer lost his life. Though his footballing career was not an illustrious one, it seems only right for him to be remembered in these pages since his name has otherwise been so totally appropriated by the fictional character he now shares it with: Harry Potter. Potter was born in Bradford on 24 November 1884, and between 1906 and 1910 he played for the Bradford City reserve team as a half-back. He does not seem to have had quite the effortless talent that some of the players mentioned in this book possessed, as during that time he failed to break into the first team. In 1910 he transferred to Lincoln City, but he remained stuck on the reserve team for the duration of his time with the club.

Because of this, Potter always had to work a full-time job during the years he was playing, first as a labourer at a dyers' and later for a fabric company. Perhaps he was determined to keep trying to progress, or perhaps he just played for sheer love of the game.

With the arrival of war Harry joined the colours with the West Yorkshire Regiment, but he was subsequently transferred to the 2/4th Battalion Lincolnshire Regiment as part of a draft of reinforcements. Harry saw action at Polygon Wood, and then at Bourlon Wood when the Germans counter-attacked following the battle of Cambrai. During both engagements his battalion suffered heavy casualties. When the decision was taken to reorganise the British Expeditionary Force in 1918, the under-strength 2/4th Lincolns were merged with the similarly depleted 1/4th Lincolns to become the 4th Lincolns.

Harry was in reserve with this newly formed battalion when the Germans began their all-out assault on 21 March, and he came under fire in the opening barrage. When the infantry attack came, the 4th Lincolns were ordered forward to help stem this seemingly unstoppable tide. Over the next two days they were one of the many battalions who were defiantly fighting a losing battle, determined to make the Germans pay for every inch they advanced. By night-time a crushing 75 per cent of their number were casualties, but they had somehow managed to keep the Germans back from their position near Vraucourt.

They were relieved that night but the next day were back out in the thick of things, still trying to protect Vraucourt. Potter and his comrades were outnumbered and in spite of their valiant efforts were unable to prevent the Germans from breaking through on their flank. They were twice forced to retreat, eventually taking to the high ground to the east of the village of Mory. It was here that the 4th Lincolns made a heroic last stand. Against the odds they somehow managed to check the German advance, but at great cost to themselves. Harry Potter was one of the battalion's many losses that day. His body, like many others, was left behind as the British troops were forced into a fighting retreat by the German war machine.

A few days later, Walter Tull and the rest of the 23rd Middlesex had to face the German onslaught. They had only just returned to France after a spell on the Italian Front, where they had been sent in November 1917 just after Passchendaele. There, Walter had proven beyond doubt that his superiors had been right to ignore the regulations prohibiting the commissioning of non-white officers. On 24 December he had led a party of twenty-six men on a reconnaissance mission across the Piave River, which separated the British and Italian forces in that area from the German and Austro-Hungarian forces. Under cover of night, Walter and his team crossed the fast-flowing river in order to ascertain the position and strength of the enemy. All bridges in the surrounding area were heavily guarded, and yet Walter returned all of his men unharmed – and with crucial intelligence.

A week later, they repeated the same journey, although this time their mission was to launch an assault on the opposite bank of the river. Again, Walter led his men with great courage and the mission was a success – the 23rd Middlesex took up positions on both banks of the river, capturing a crucial bridge in the process and taking several prisoners. For his leadership in both crossings of the Piave, Walter was mentioned in dispatches by his commanding officer, Major General Sydney Lawford, who praised him for his 'gallantry and coolness'.

Following this promising start to his career as an officer, in March 1918 Walter Tull was recalled to northern France with the rest of 23rd Middlesex. The battalion had just set up camp in Favreuil, a small town just south of Arras, when the German attack began. After several days of systematically forcing British troops into retreat, German forces finally struck in the area where the 23rd Middlesex were stationed.

It quickly became clear to Walter that he and his men were being overwhelmed. He was shouting commands, desperately trying to marshal his men in order to consolidate their defences against the onslaught, when a machine-gun bullet hit him in the side of the neck. He died almost instantly. Several attempts were made by his men to recover his body from where he fell in no man's land – former Leicester Fosse goalkeeper Tom Billingham among them – but the danger posed by the enemy meant they had to give up. At twenty-nine years old, Walter found his final resting place out on the fields of France.

Just over three weeks later, Walter's brother Edward was at his home in Glasgow when he received the telegram he had long dreaded, informing him of his brother's death. It was followed by a letter from Lieutenant Pickard, Walter's fellow officer in the 23rd Middlesex, which read as follows:

Of course you have already heard of the death of 2nd Lieut. W. D. Tull on March 25th last.

Being at present in command of 'C' Co. – (the Captain was wounded) – allow me to say how popular he was throughout the Battalion. He was brave and conscientious; he had been recommended for the Military Cross, and had certainly earned it; the Commanding Officer had every confidence in him, and he was liked by the men.

Now he has paid the supreme sacrifice 'pro patria'; the Battalion and Company have lost a faithful officer; personally, I have lost a friend. Can I say more! Except that I hope that those who remain may be as true and faithful as he.

Lieutenant Pickard's letter serves as testament to the strength of character of a man who overcame the obstacles that racial discrimination laid before him, both in his career as a footballer and as the first black combat officer in the British army. Even without having to contend with the difficulties he did, his achievements would still have been remarkable. Tull's name is inscribed on the Arras Memorial for those who have no known grave. In 1999 his former club Northampton Town unveiled a memorial and garden of remembrance in his honour. The memorial is inscribed with the following words:

Through his actions, W. D. J. Tull ridiculed the barriers of ignorance that tried to deny people of colour equality with their contemporaries. His life stands testament to a determination to confront those people and those obstacles that sought to diminish him and the world in which he lived. It reveals a man, though rendered breathless in his prime, whose strong heart still beats loudly.

The first few days of Ludendorff's Spring Offensive had swept aside resistance and allowed the German army to advance miles. So successful were the first few days of the attack, in fact, that the kaiser declared 24 March a national holiday. It really looked as though the quick victory they needed might be within their grasp. However, in order to move with such speed the German forward troops had deliberately carried very little with them. As the advance rushed on, the supply units at the rear were left behind. The units leading the attack began to run out of vital supplies.

This proved to be fatal for the continued progress of the attack. Ludendorff wanted his forces to attack and capture the city of Amiens, which was a major rail centre for the Allies; failing to do so would be a severe blow. The German general was completely right in this, but he had failed to take into account how severe the supply problems were and the effect that this would have on the troops. Before attacking Amiens, the German forces went to Albert. Here the desperate, hungry German soldiers were confronted with shops full of food. It's hardly surprising that discipline broke down at once and the men began to loot the city. The commanders were unable to regain control of their men and as a result the attack on Amiens stuttered to a halt.

On 5 April Ludendorff officially called off the advance. It had indeed been a swift and deadly attack that the Allies had found almost impossible to resist. But it had failed to deal any decisive blows. True, the sheer amount of land that German forces had managed to seize as they drove the Allies back through France was incredibly impressive. However, for all that, vital positions such as Amiens remained in Allied hands. In addition to this, the territorial gains had actually considerably extended the line that the Germans would have to hold now that the attack had petered out. The Allies had suffered 255,000 casualties over the course of the attack but Germany had suffered almost as many itself – 239,000 in total. While the Allies could at least hope that the gaps left would be filled by the influx of American soldiers to the continent, Germany could expect no such reinforcements. Furthermore, German losses had naturally been heaviest for those units leading the assault, meaning that many of their best troops had been lost, including the irreplaceable storm troop units.

Ludendorff's plan had not been a success but, having committed themselves, the Germans had no choice but to continue their aggressive strategy in the hope that they might still snatch victory before it was too late. Over the next few months the Germans undertook several more concerted attacks, but the Allies continued to hold on tenaciously to vital locations while allowing the Germans to gain worthless land, thereby continuing to stretch their supply lines and overextend themselves.

The final significant German offensive took place on 15 July, east of the city of Reims. The fighting that ensued is usually referred to as the Second Battle of the Marne (the First Battle of the Marne had occurred in the area in September 1914). Although they made some headway on the first day of this offensive, on the second the Germans were brought to a standstill by French defenders supported by British and American troops. Then on 18 July a predominantly French force, including around 350 tanks, counter-attacked and managed to overwhelm the right flank of the German forces. They were driven back, sustaining severe casualties in the process. As a result of this, on 20 July General Ludendorff ordered his forces into retreat. It was a severe blow; for a time their sustained offences had been a real danger to the Allies, but with this reversal the immediate prospect of a German victory had passed. Since the beginning of their attacks back in March, the Germans had suffered in the region of a million casualties. The scales were tipping in the Allies' favour – now it was their turn to go on the offensive.

On 8 August the Allies attacked close to Amiens. The British Fourth Army struck first, forgoing the traditional artillery bombardment in order to achieve the element of surprise. They relied instead on tanks and a creeping barrage that accompanied the attack itself. At the same time, the French began a bombardment from their part of the line and – when this had softened resistance just forty-five minutes later – joined in the attack. The Germans were swept away, and the Allies broke through to advance an average of seven miles on the first day alone. By 11 August the Germans had been pushed back to the positions they had occupied at the start of the Spring Offensive. A massive 74,000 casualties had been sustained by the Germans, against

22,000 Allied casualties. German morale seemed to be wavering, with many units surrendering to Allied forces with very little resistance. Ludendorff himself described the Battle of Amiens as 'the blackest day of the German Army'.

The war had now truly become a moving conflict once again, in contrast to the slow attritional trench warfare that had been dominating the past years. Over the rest of the summer the Allies pushed the Germans back across France, the British expelling them from the north, the French and Americans from the south. By 2 September the Germans were forced to retreat once more behind their greatest defence, the Hindenburg Line. But the Allied commanders would no longer be deterred – they had their enemy on the ropes. On 26 September they launched a 'grand offensive' against the German fortifications, masterminded by Marshal Foch, the Frenchman who had been appointed as overarching generalissimo of all Allied forces. Which brings us to the last of the footballers whose story will be told in this book. Although his career as a player ended somewhat abortively, his achievements during the war were among the most remarkable. His name was Bernard William Vann.

*

Bernard Vann was born on 9 July 1887 in Rushden, Northamptonshire, to Alfred George Collins Vann and his wife Hannah Elizabeth. Both of his parents taught at South End Elementary School, which Bernard and his four brothers all attended. While Bernard did not follow in his parents' academic footsteps – a wonderfully frank article in his student newspaper described Bernard's contributions to the debating society as 'quite untrammelled by any consideration of grammatical lucidity' – his prowess on the sports field was undeniable, and he was soon made captain of the school's hockey, cricket and football teams.

Upon leaving school, Bernard turned out for the Leicestershire county hockey team, but soon turned his attention towards football. In 1905 the eighteen-year-old started his career as an amateur centre forward at Northampton Town, the club where his brother Albert played. His first season with Northampton was fairly unremarkable, with his talents only being called upon twice, but in the 1906–07 season he managed five goals in five games. His consistency was noted by the management at Burton United (a Second Division team at the time), who promptly snapped him up. Bernard made twelve appearances for the club before he moved once again, this time to First Division Derby County.

Derby's manager at the time, Jimmy Methven, had made a remarkable 458 appearances for the Rams between 1891 and 1906, when he turned his hand to management instead. His first season in this new role had not been easy, however, with the team winning only seven of their first thirty games. In March 1907, with only eight games left to turn the club's fortunes around, Methven turned to Bernard Vann.

This was Vann's first season in the First Division, and his task was unenviable. On Saturday 23 March, he made his debut against Aston Villa, who had previously beaten Derby 1-0 at the Baseball Ground (Derby's home from 1895 to 1997). Away at Villa Park, the Rams fared no better, losing the game 2-0. The following Friday, Bernard made his second appearance for the club, this time against a Notts County team who were also languishing perilously close to the relegation zone. Going into this game, Bernard and the rest of the team could at least take comfort in the knowledge that last time they had played Notts County they had emerged as clear victors, scoring three goals and keeping a clean sheet.

However, Notts County were out for revenge and desperate to secure their position in the First Division. Even with Bernard's talents in attack to call upon, Derby found it impossible to break through the Magpies' determined defence, while they themselves conceded goal after goal. It must have been a painful match; by the end, the score stood at 4-0 to Notts County. Derby's season didn't recover after this drubbing, and Vann only made one more appearance, in a 1-1 draw against Birmingham. The Rams finished the season nineteenth in the league and were subsequently relegated to the Second Division.

After this disappointing introduction to First Division football, Bernard decided to take a break from the game and went to study at Cambridge. In fact, this was to be the end of his career in the national game; he left college in 1910, having realised that he wanted his life to take a different path – he became a junior curate at St Barnabas Church, Leicester, in November that same year. Though this constituted a fairly drastic change in career path, it was not entirely without precedent in the family; Bernard's uncle, the Reverend Thomas Simpson, was also a member of the clergy. Vann spent the next two years at St Barnabas, and was ordained into the priesthood in January 1912. Following his ordination he became a chaplain at Wellingborough School where, ever tireless, he instructed classes in theology and history and coached both the football and cricket teams. He continued to play football himself, apparently with gusto – in October 1912 he was severely concussed during a game at Oundle School and had to stay in bed for a week.

Immediately after the outbreak of the war in August 1914, Bernard applied to become an army chaplain. However, the application process took far too long for his liking, and Bernard wasn't willing to sit around waiting while his countrymen were in the thick of things. Barely four weeks after England had declared war on Germany, Bernard signed up as a private with the Artists Rifles and was then quickly commissioned into the 1/8th Battalion Sherwood Foresters as an officer. The 27-year-old footballer-priest arrived in France as a second lieutenant in February 1915, having gained the single Bath star.

Vann took to his new role with characteristic alacrity, and immediately gained a reputation for being a fearless and well-liked officer. While stationed with the 1/8th Sherwood Foresters near Kemmel, West Flanders, Vann underwent his first traumatic front-line experience when the battalion's position came under attack by German artillery on 24 April. The trench they were occupying caved in, leaving Vann and many others wounded and half buried. Vann managed to dig himself out of the collapsed trench and, once he had done so, refused to leave his post in spite of being wounded. The bombardment only lasted an hour, but left fourteen men of the 1/8th Sherwood Foresters dead and sixteen wounded. Vann was later commended for his efforts in organising the defence of the battalion's position, as well as for rescuing several wounded comrades.

This incident, in addition to several daring reconnaissance missions he conducted when the 1/8th were stationed at Ypres in July, led to Vann being awarded the Military Cross that August, as well as being promoted to the rank of lieutenant. But the following month, tragedy befell the Vann family when Bernard's brother Albert (who had also been his Northampton Town teammate) was killed during the Battle of Loos. Albert had been a captain with the 12th Battalion West Yorkshire Regiment at the time of his death, and was one of sixteen officers and 300 other ranks from the battalion to be killed or wounded at Loos.

Bernard Vann's full-blooded commitment to his duties was in no way diminished by the news of his brother's death, and over the following months he continued to demonstrate the bravery for which he was becoming renowned. In the process he incurred several injuries, including a particularly severe one during

the Battle of the Hohenzollern Redoubt. While leading an assault on the German positions in the early
hours of 14 October, a bullet went clean through his
left forearm, exiting below the elbow and damaging
the radial nerve in the process. In spite of this, Vann
continued to use his good arm to throw grenades, until
his commanding officer ordered that he withdraw to
be treated. In spite of the serious nature of his injury,
Vann made as full a recovery as could have been hoped
for, and following a brief spell in training he was back
on the front line by March 1916.

During the course of 1916 Bernard received further
distinctions, as he was promoted first to captain and
then to acting major, roles he took up with his cus-
tomary enthusiasm and vigour. On the night of 21
September, Vann led his men in a raid on an enemy
sap in Bellacourt, Rivière (a sap was a shallow trench
created as a forward position ahead of the main front-
line defences). They first fired on the sap with trench
mortars in order to create gaps in the enemy wire.
Following this, under cover of machine-gun fire, a
wire patrol set out to confirm that the gaps were large
enough and to lay tape from them back to the Allied
front line in order to guide the raiding party. Once
this was done, having blackened their hands, faces

and bayonets – and removed all rank insignia and any other identifying marks in case of falling into enemy hands – Vann and his men set out at 12.15 a.m. under the cover of a creeping barrage. As soon as this lifted at 12.28 a.m., the raiding party poured through the gaps in the wire and assaulted the enemy line. Vann came upon a dugout full of German soldiers, whom he ordered to come out and surrender. Upon hearing his voice, two of them rushed out with their bayonets fixed. Keeping his cool, Vann killed one and wounded the other, causing the rest to promptly surrender. The raiding party returned to their own lines triumphant, having killed five of the enemy and captured five more.

For his courage in the raid, Vann was awarded a bar to his Military Cross, and later the French Croix de Guerre (avec palme). The official citation for the former read: 'for conspicuous gallantry in action. He led a daring raid against the enemy's trenches, himself taking five prisoners and displaying great courage and determination. He has on many previous occasions done fine work.'

However, Vann had sustained yet more injuries in the process. The cumulative effect, in addition to the neuritis caused by his previous injury, led to Vann being sent back to Britain to recuperate for the rest

of 1916. While back home, he attended the Senior
Officers' School in Aldershot. He also found the time
to propose to Doris Victoria Beck, a twenty-year-
old nursing aide from Ontario, Canada. Doris had
travelled to London in order to work at St Dunstan's, a
military charity established in 1915 to care for the huge
numbers of blinded servicemen who were returning
from the battlefields of France. Happily, Doris accepted
the proposal and she and Bernard were married on 27
December 1916 at St Paul's Church in Knightsbridge.

By Vann's standards, 1917 was a quiet year. Most of
the first part was spent in preparation for assuming
command of the 1/6th Battalion Sherwood Foresters in
September, where he gained a promotion to the rank
of acting lieutenant colonel a month later. For the next
five months, Vann and the men of the 1/6th were mostly
occupied with training. However, in spring 1918, when
the Russians pulled out of the war, the 1/6th Sherwood
Foresters were under no illusions as to what this would
mean for them. An entry in their war diary from the
time reads:

As a result of the withdrawal of Russia from the war,
and the consequent release of German troops from
the Russian front, everything pointed to the Allies

on the Western front being on the defensive for some considerable time…Much open warfare and trench-to-trench attack practice was carried out, a very ominous sign being that this consisted mainly of counter-attacks to regain portions of trenches lost!

In response to the increased threat, from March to September 1918 Vann and his men moved between various weakened sections of the Allied front line, offering relief for their weary colleagues as the Allies first struggled against the Spring Offensive and then strove to drive the Germans out of France. At last, having fought and served at Cambrin, Lens, Gorre and Cuinchy, the 1/6th were moved to the region of the St Quentin Canal. It was for his actions while his battalion was part of an Allied attack here on 29 September that Vann earned himself the highest military distinction of all.

During the attack, Bernard and his men crossed the canal at Bellenglise and Lehaucourt. They were shrouded in thick fog but nonetheless found themselves under heavy fire. With the advance held up, there was a danger that the British soldiers would lose the benefit of the creeping barrage from their own artillery that was sweeping forward with them. Vann therefore courageously led his men forward in order to attack a battery of field guns. What happened next is described in the citation for the Victoria Cross he would later be awarded:

> For most conspicuous bravery, devotion to Duty and fine leadership during the attack at Bellenglise and Lehaucourt on 29th September 1918. He led his battalion with great skill across the St Quentin Canal through a very thick fog and heavy fire from field and machine guns. On reaching the high ground above Bellenglise, the whole attack was held up by fire of all descriptions from the front and right flank. Realizing that everything depended on the advance going forward with the barrage, Lt. Col. Vann rushed up to the firing line, and with the greatest gallantry led the line forward. By his prompt action and contempt for danger the whole situation was changed, the men were encouraged and the line swept forward. Later he rushed a field gun single handed, and knocked out three of the detachment. The success of the day was in no small degree due to the splendid gallantry and fine leadership displayed by this officer.

Tragically, Vann would not live to hear of being

awarded the VC. On 3 October 1918 he was shot and killed by a German sniper while his battalion was waiting in readiness to attack the Fonsomme–Beaurevoir line (also known as the Hindenburg Support Line). He would have been proud to know that his men went on to capture their objectives that day, even without his inspiring leadership.

Bernard Vann was thirty-one years old when he lost his life in the line of duty. Vann was the only clergyman ordained in the Church of England to win a Victoria Cross as a combatant in the First World War. His posthumous medal also made him the most decorated man who had played for a First Division football club; though since he was never paid, not the most decorated professional player – that honour belongs to Donald Simpson Bell (see page 19).

Perhaps the most tragic postscript to Bernard Vann's story is that on 29 June 1919 his widow Doris gave birth to a son, also named Bernard Vann. This baby must have been conceived just weeks before his father's death, most likely during ten days of leave that Bernard spent in Paris with Doris; the last time they ever saw each other. Bernard Vann – footballer, clergyman and war hero – is buried in France in the Bellicourt British Cemetery.

Vann's death is rendered all the more frustrating by

the fact that, at this point, it was clear that the Allies were going to win the war. By 29 September, Allied forces had already broken through the Hindenburg Line. Both General Ludendorff and Field Marshal Hindenburg had already informed Kaiser Wilhelm that victory was no longer possible, and that they should sue for peace. In spite of this, the fighting went on throughout October while the German army continued to retreat back across the territory they had gained at the very start of the war, fighting fierce rearguard actions even as morale crumbled. Yet more casualties were sustained on both sides. Germany itself teetered on the brink of revolution.

Finally, on 9 November 1918 it was announced that Kaiser Wilhelm had abdicated and that the terms of an armistice had been agreed, to take effect in two days. On the eleventh hour, of the eleventh day, of the eleventh month, the guns finally fell silent in Europe. The First World War was over; after four long years of bitter conflict, Britain and her Allies were victorious.

For many it must have felt a hollow victory. A quarter of a million British people were dead, and for other countries the toll was much higher. In total the war had killed more than sixteen million people, and left millions more with serious injuries of both mind and body. The British footballers included in that appalling number are but a minute fraction of the total, yet their stories demand our attention.

Perhaps it is the very nature of football – a competition in which two opposing sides strive against each other for victory – that gives their stories such fascination and pathos. In the end, for all that it is vast, ugly and cruel, what is war but another such competition? We instinctively recoil from the fact that these men in the prime of life were forced to abandon a competitive sport – which, at its best, can build bonds of community and humanity – in order to take part in a conflict that did nothing but tear such bonds apart. And yet we cannot fail to be filled with admiration at the way they conducted themselves in such circumstances; as a tribute later published by Arsenal has it: 'In civil life they were heroes and they proved themselves heroes on the battlefield.'

On 10 March 1924 the then-president of the FA unveiled a memorial tablet attached to the FA offices in Russell Square, commemorating all the professional and amateur footballers who fell during the First World War. Though this is no longer in place, many more memorials have since been erected in honour of the footballing heroes who served from 1914–18.

A memorial for Donald Simpson Bell was unveiled in Contalmaison in July 2000. Situated at Bell's Redoubt (see page 141), the memorial includes a bronze replica of the wooden cross originally laid by the men of Bell's battalion. Those who served in McCrae's battalion, the 16th Royal Scots, are similarly commemorated in Contalmaison, with a memorial cairn which was unveiled in November 2004; some eighty-five years after it was first proposed.

In October 2010, a memorial was erected in Longueval to the men of the 17th and 23rd Middlesex. Situated just south-east of Delville Wood, the memorial serves as a powerful reminder of those men who, when called upon by their country, left behind the fierce rivalries of club football to stand united, fighting side by side in the trenches.

It has been impossible to include all the Association Football players who fought in the First World War within these pages. Nor does this book have the permanence of being written in stone. However, it is the hope of the author that it may also serve as some small memorial for a collection of men who stood out even by the standards of their extraordinary generation.

We will remember them.

Bibliography

Books

Alexander, J., *McCrae's Battalion: The Story of the 16th Royal Scots* (Mainstream Publishing, 2003)

Bell, M., *Red White and Khaki: The Story of the Only Wartime FA Cup Final* (Peakpublish, 2011)

Brown, M., & Seaton, S., *The Christmas Truce: The Western Front December 1914* (Pan Grand Strategy, 2001)

Creagh, G., & Humphris, E. M., *The V.C. and D.S.O.: Volume 1, The Victoria Cross* (The Standard Art Book Company, 1924)

Gliddon, G., *VCs of the First World War: Somme 1916* (The History Press, 2011)

Gliddon, G., *When the Barrage Lifts: Topographical History and Commentary on the Battle of the Somme, 1916* (Gliddon Books, 1987)

Harris, C., and Whippy, J., *The Greater Game: Sporting Icons Who Fell in the Great War* (Pen and Sword, 2008)

Jenkins, S., *They Took the Lead: The Story of Clapton Orient's*

Major Contribution to the Footballers' Battalion in the Great War (DDP One Stop UK, 2006)

Matthews, T., *England's Who's Who: One Hundred and Forty Years of English International Footballers 1872–2013* (Pitch Publishing, 2013)

Middlebrook, M., *The First Day on the Somme* (Pen and Sword Books, 2002)

Riddoch, A., & Kemp, J., *When the Whistle Blows: The Story of the Footballers' Battalion in the Great War* (Hayes, 2008)

Sanders, R., *Beastly Fury: The Strange Birth of British Football* (Bantam Books, 2009)

Tait, C. S., *Stones in the Millpond – Reflections on the First World War* (Shetland Library, 2001)

Terret, T., & Mangan, J. A. (eds.), *Sport, Militarism and the Great War: Martial Manliness and Armageddon* (Routledge, 2012)

Vignes, S., *Lost in France: The Remarkable Life and Death of Leigh Richmond Roose, Football's First Playboy* (Stadia, 2007)

Vasili, P., *Walter Tull (1888–1918), Officer, Footballer: All the Guns in France Couldn't Wake Me* (Raw Press, 2009)

Wall, F., *Fifty Years of Football: 1895–1934* (Cassell, 1935)

Westlake, R., *British Battalions in France and Belgium, 1914* (Pen and Sword Books, 1997)

Websites

The Long, Long Trail – www.1914-1918.net
The Football Association – www.thefa.co.uk
The Commonwealth War Graves Commission – www.cwgc.org

Acknowledgements

I could not have written this book without the help and support of a great many people and organisations, to whom I am indebted. My thanks are due first of all to Gary Lineker for so graciously providing a foreword, as well as to his agent Jon Holmes.

For their help and guidance I am extremely grateful to Neil Thornton, Phil Stant, Alan Clay, Hal Giblin, Roy Mitchell, William Ivory and Philip Nodding. I must also mention the staff of the following institutions, who were greatly supportive: the National Football Museum (especially Dr Alexander Jackson, Collections Officer), the Football League and the Football Association.

Thanks to my agent Robert Kirby, as well as to

the editorial team at Random House Books: Nigel Wilcockson, Fred Baty, and in particular my friend and editor Harry Scoble.

Finally, and most importantly, my thanks are due to the footballing heroes who are the subjects of this book: to the men of the 17th and 23rd Middlesex; to Sir George McCrae and the 16th Royal Scots; to Donald Simpson Bell, William Angus, Bernard Vann, Sandy Turnbull, Walter Tull, William Jonas, Richard McFadden, and the countless others who served, and fell, in the Great War. They are a constant source of inspiration.

Index

INDEX